# Origami

# Sticky Note

# Origami

## DAVID MITCHELL

## COLLINS & BROWN

Produced in 2005 by
PRC Publishing
The Chrysalis Building
Bramley Road, London W10 6SP

An imprint of **Chrysalis** Books Group plc

First published in Great Britain in 2005 by
Collins & Brown
The Chrysalis Building
Bramley Road, London W10 6SP

An imprint of **Chrysalis** Books Group plc

1 2 3 4 5 6 7 8 9

ISBN: 1 84340 227 0

Printed in Malaysia

# Contents

# Introduction

Origami, or paperfolding, is a modern phenomenon with ancient roots. It is impossible to say when and where paper was first folded, or who it was that first discovered that paperfolding could be more than just a practical way to prevent furniture rocking. But what we do know is that today's paperfolders will happily fold virtually anything, anywhere: Paris Metro tickets, advertising flyers, teabag labels, business cards and so on. It is therefore not surprising that paperfolders should also have begun to explore the folding potential of that other modern phenomenon, the sticky note, which provides some unique design surprises of its own.

Sticky notes are small colorful pieces of paper bearing an adhesive strip along one edge. The secret of their success lies in the nature of the adhesive strip. In 1968, Dr. Spencer Silver, a research scientist working for the 3M

Corporation, developed acrylate copolymer microspheres, an entirely new adhesive. He could, however, find no practical purpose for his discovery, since his new adhesive was exceptionally weak, and strong adhesives were the order of the day. It was not until 1974 that one of his colleagues, Art Fry, realized that since the glue did not damage or mark surfaces it was attached to, even easily friable surfaces like paper, it could be used to make a kind of reusable bookmark. This idea was gradually developed into the ubiquitous sticky notes we know today, which were first marketed in 1977.

To many modern paperfolders the challenge of origami design lies in producing a design from just a single sheet of paper by folding alone, eschewing the use of cuts or decoration of any kind. Some paperfolders go even further than this and insist on only working from plain paper squares. This kind of origami is known as pure origami, and it undoubtedly has its place. But its place is not here. Sticky note origami is by definition impure—but this doesn't make it any less fun.

At its best, origami design makes use of every quality of the material being folded, and one of the most obvious qualities of sticky notes is that they come complete with an adhesive strip. The origami designs in this book aim to make the fullest possible use of this unique and interesting feature. The adhesive strip is used to enable you to attach sticky note origami designs to suitable surfaces like walls, partitions and VDU screens. It is also used to attach parts of designs to each other to create larger multi-piece and modular forms, and even to create compound sheets that can be used in traditional types of origami design. As far as origami goes, there is, as this book shows, little that can not be done with sticky notes and a little ingenuity. The main limiting factor is the size of the notes, which militate against complexity. Consequently, the designs

included in this book are necessarily simple, but this should be seen as a bonus rather than a disadvantage.

Sticky notes come in many sizes and shapes, but the designs in this book have been developed from the three most commonly available types of notes: small 3:4 rectangles of 1.5" x 2" (38mm x 51mm) dimensions, large squares of 3" (76mm) dimensions, and large 3:5 rectangles of 3" x 5" (76mm x 127mm) dimensions. All of these sizes of note are easily available from local stationery suppliers or mail-order outlets in blocks of many attractive and exciting colors. And, as sticky notes are usually close at hand in offices, you should never find yourself with a dull moment at work again!

# Understanding Origami Diagrams

Origami diagrams are a kind of musical score for origami, a sequence of "before" and "after" pictures that allow paperfolding designers to record their designs, and other paperfolders to reproduce those designs for themselves.

Each picture in the diagrams is numbered to show the sequence in which they should be read. The "before" pictures are marked with folding symbols that show you which part of the paper moves during the fold, where it ends up, and where the crease will form. The "after" pictures show you what the paper will look like once the fold has been made.

The secret of reading diagrams is to always look one step ahead. If you know what the result of the fold should look like before you start to make it you are much more likely to get it right first time. Here are "before" and "after" pictures for a simple fold:

**1.** Fold in half from right to left. Picture 2 shows what the result should look like.

**2.** This is the result.

The words provide a quick explanation of what the picture is telling you to do. The words are useful, especially at first, but the pictures contain more information and you should try to get used to relying on them as quickly as you can. A full explanation of picture 1 in words would go something like this, "Pick up the left hand edge, curl it over until it lies exactly on top of the right hand edge, hold it in place and flatten it down so that a sharp crease forms." You will notice that although the two edges should be folded exactly onto each other picture 2 actually shows them slightly out of line. This is because you will often need to know how many layers of paper you should have along each edge, and this slight distortion is the only way to show it clearly.

In order to save on the number of diagrams required to explain a design, each "after" diagram is usually also the "before" diagram for the next step in the sequence.

Note that in the diagrams below the "after" picture, step 2, has changed. Step 2

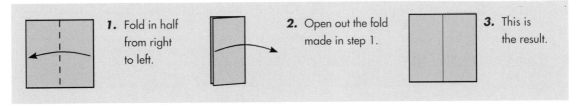

**1.** Fold in half from right to left.

**2.** Open out the fold made in step 1.

**3.** This is the result.

not only shows the result of step 1 but also gives instructions for the next fold, in this case telling you that the fold should be opened out again. Step 3 shows the result of this. The crease made in step 1 is shown as a thin line in step 3.

To save even more space pictures 1 and 2 would normally be combined into a single fold/crease/unfold instruction that would look like this:

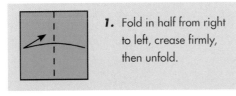

**1.** Fold in half from right to left, crease firmly, then unfold.

# A Guide to the Folding Diagrams and Symbols

Here is a visual dictionary explaining the meaning of all the symbols you will come across while following the folding instructions in this book.

Edges that lie exactly on top of each other as the result of a fold are normally shown slightly offset on the after diagram.

The edges of the paper are shown as solid lines.

A movement arrow without a fold-line means unfold in the direction indicated.

A folding instruction consists of a movement arrow and a fold-line.

Creases you have already made are shown as thin lines.

The movement arrow shows the direction in which the fold is made.

This version of the fold arrow means fold, crease firmly, then unfold.

The fold-line shows where the new crease will form. A dashed fold-line means the fold is made toward you.

A dashed and dotted fold-line means that the fold should be made away from you.

Different tints are sometimes used to distinguish one side of the paper from the other.

 A diagram of this kind tells you to swivel the flap to the back by reversing the direction of the existing crease.

 Dotted lines are used to show hidden or imaginary lines, such as edges of the paper, shafts of fold-arrows, or the edge of an adhesive strip where they lie, or pass, out of sight underneath the top surface of the paper.

 This symbol shows how the adjacent edge can be seen as divided into a number of equal sections to help you locate a fold.

 This combination of symbols shows you how existing creases can be used to collapse the paper into a different shape.

 This symbol tells you to apply gentle pressure to the paper in the direction the arrowhead is pointing.

 This symbol tells you to move the paper gently in the direction of the arrow.

 This symbol tells you to turn the paper over sideways.

 This symbol indicates that the next diagram is on a larger scale.

 A circle is used to draw attention to some particular part of a picture referred to in the text.

# Elephants Extreme

DESIGNED BY DAVID MITCHELL

There are many different styles of origami design, each of which offers its own particular challenge and reward. Sometimes designers work hard to make their models realistically complex, so that every detail is portrayed as accurately as possible. At other times they work equally hard to suggest their subject in the absolute minimum number of folds. Even so, very few minimalist designs are quite as simple as Elephants Extreme. It doesn't seem possible that the body, ears, and trunk of an elephant could be suggested in just three, or even, quite absurdly, just one, fold. But it is.

These simple designs translate quite wonderfully into the new world of sticky note origami design. Want to leave a "Don't forget …" reminder for someone that will stand out from the crowd? Either of these Elephants Extreme designs will do the job.

**Requirements:** You will need just one sticky note of any color for each design. 3" x 5" (76mm x 127mm) notes are ideal, but the design will work from many other rectangles as well.

**1.**

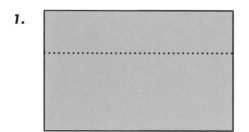

**3.**

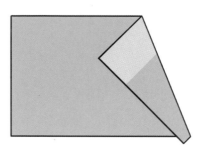

**2.**

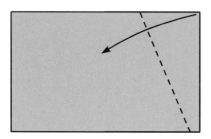

**4.**

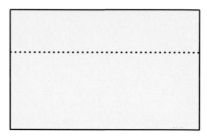

### 1-FOLD ELEPHANT

Begin with a 3" x 5" (76mm x 127mm) note arranged in the way shown in picture 1, so that the adhesive strip is not visible.

**1.** The dotted line marks the position of the edge of the adhesive strip.

**2.** Make a single fold as shown. Note that in order to avoid the trunk ending in a point the crease does not go through the bottom right-hand corner.

**3.** The 1-fold Elephant is finished. This is probably the simplest design in the origami repertoire.

### 3-FOLD ELEPHANT

If the 1-fold Elephant is just too extreme for your taste, you may like to try this slightly more realistic variation. Begin with the note arranged in the way shown in picture 4, so that the adhesive strip is not visible.

**4.** The dotted line marks the position of the edge of the adhesive strip.

**5.**

**6.**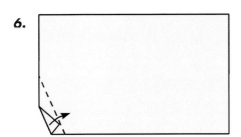

**7.**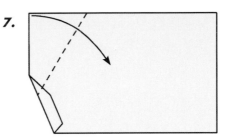

**8.**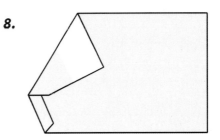

**5.** Make a very tiny first fold as shown.

**6.** The second fold creates the lower half of the trunk.

**7.** The third fold creates the upper half of the trunk and suggests the ears.

**8.** The 3-fold Elephant is finished.

# Butterflies

DESIGNED BY DAVID MITCHELL

Butterflies are among the earliest known origami designs. In ancient Japan, male and female butterflies, known as Ocho and Mecho, were used to decorate the necks of sake bottles during marriage ceremonies from very early times.

Butterflies can be made from almost any shape of rectangular notes. Like traditional Japanese origami butterflies they also come in male and female varieties, both of which can be folded equally easily from the same size and shape of rectangular note. When the butterflies are finished you can use the exposed part of the adhesive to attach them to any suitable surface, such as windows, partitions or VDU screens, or even a sake bottle, if you happen to have one handy. Sticky note butterflies can also be used to add an eye-catching decorative touch to that important message.

**Requirements:** You will need one 1.5" x 2" (38mm x 51mm) note of any color for each butterfly.

**1.**

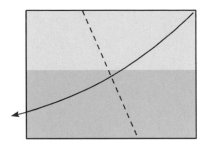

**2.**

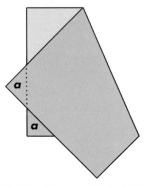

**3.**

**4.**

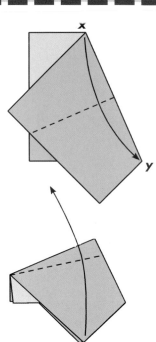

### FOLDING THE FEMALE BUTTERFLY

Begin with a 1.5″ x 2″ (38mm x 51mm) note of any bright color arranged in the way shown in picture 1 so that the adhesive strip is visible.

**1.** Make this fold so that the result looks as much as possible like picture 2, but do not crease it firmly yet.

**2.** Adjust your fold so that the two small triangular areas marked **a** are the same size and shape. Crease firmly.

**3.** Fold point **x** onto point **y**. Crease firmly.

**4.** Fold one wing upward to form one half of the body of the butterfly. You can vary the position of this fold to produce a slightly fatter or thinner body. Picture 5 shows what the result should look like.

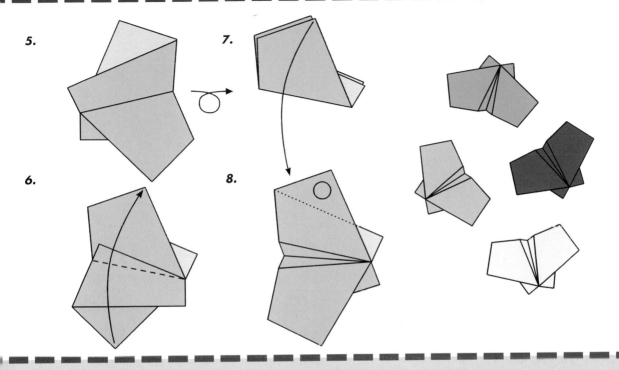

**5.** This is the result. Turn over sideways.

**6.** Fold the second wing upward in a similar way. Make sure that the edges of both wings lie exactly on top of each other.

**7.** Open out the folds made in steps 4 and 6, without completely flattening the creases, to reveal the finished female butterfly.

**8.** The female butterfly is finished. The underside of the triangular area marked with a circle is sticky and can be used to attach the butterfly to any suitable flat surface (such as a VDU screen).

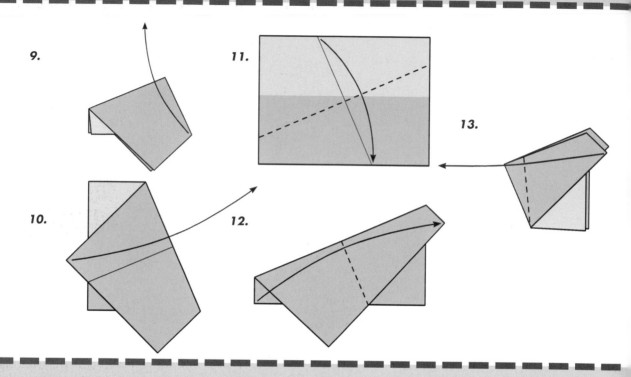

9.

10.

11.

12.

13.

**FOLDING THE MALE BUTTERFLY**

Begin by following steps 1 through 3 of the instructions for the female butterfly.

**9.** Open out the fold made in step 3.

**10.** Open out the fold made in step 1.

**11.** Use the crease created in step 3 to make this fold.

**12.** Fold in half using the crease created in step 1.

**13.** Fold one wing across to form one half of the body of the butterfly. You can vary the position of this fold to produce a slightly fatter or thinner body. Picture 14 shows what the result should look like.

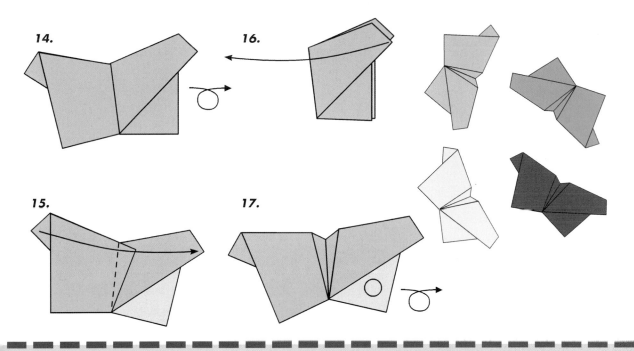

**14.** This is the result. Turn over sideways.

**15.** Fold the second wing across in a similar way. Make sure that the edges of both wings lie exactly on top of each other.

**16.** Open out the folds made in steps 13 and 15 without completely flattening the creases to reveal the finished male butterfly.

**17.** The male butterfly is finished. The triangular area marked with a circle is sticky and can be used to attach the butterfly to any suitable flat surface.

# Posy

## DESIGNED BY DAVID MITCHELL

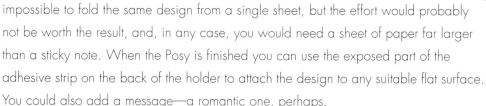

Posy is a two-piece minimalist design that suggests a bunch of flowers, or perhaps a single bloom. The advantage of combining several elements folded from individual notes into a single design is that you can use color more effectively and achieve simpler, more elegant, folding sequences. It is by no means impossible to fold the same design from a single sheet, but the effort would probably not be worth the result, and, in any case, you would need a sheet of paper far larger than a sticky note. When the Posy is finished you can use the exposed part of the adhesive strip on the back of the holder to attach the design to any suitable flat surface. You could also add a message—a romantic one, perhaps.

**Requirements:** Posy is made from two 1.5" x 2" (38mm x 51mm) notes. One should be green, to form the holder (and perhaps hint at the existence of leaves), and the other red, or some other suitably bright color, to form the flower.

**1.**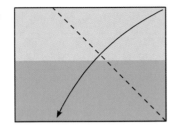

**3.**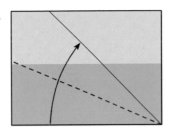

**5.**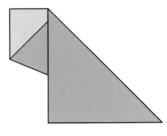

**2.**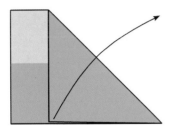

**4.**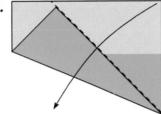

### FOLDING THE HOLDER

Begin with a green 1.5″ x 2″ (38mm x 51mm) note arranged in the way shown in picture 1, so that the adhesive strip is visible.

**1.** Fold the right-hand edge onto the bottom edge and crease firmly. Picture 2 shows what the result should look like.

**2.** Open out the fold made in step 1.

**3.** Fold the bottom edge onto the crease you made in step 1.

**4.** This is the result. Remake the fold you made in step 1 using the existing crease.

**5.** The holder is finished.

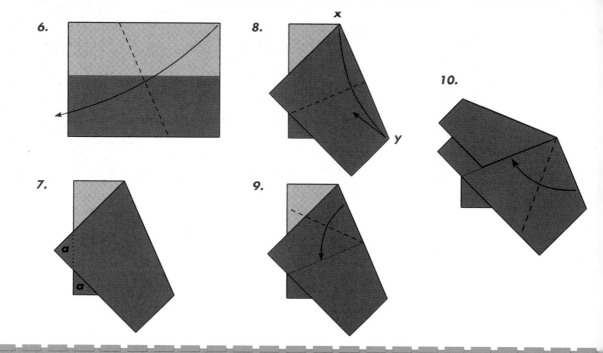

**FOLDING THE FLOWER**

Begin with a red 1.5" x 2" (38mm x 51mm) note arranged in the way shown in picture 6, so that the adhesive strip is visible.

**6.** Make this fold so that the result looks as much as possible like picture 7.

**7.** Adjust your fold so that the two small triangular areas marked *a* are the same size and shape. Crease firmly.

**8.** Fold point **x** onto point **y**, crease firmly, then unfold.

**9.** Fold the top half of the right hand edge onto the crease made in step 8. The result should look like picture 10. Crease firmly.

**10.** Fold the bottom half of the right hand edge onto the crease made in step 8. The result should look like picture 11.

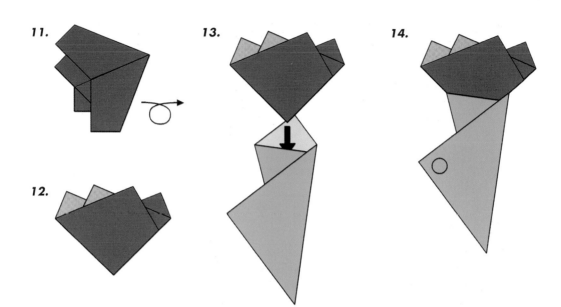

**11.** This is the result. Turn over and rotate so that the design looks like picture 12.

**12.** The flower is finished.

## ASSEMBLING THE POSY

**13.** Assemble the Posy by inserting the flower inside the layers of the holder, like this. The two elements will stick together.

**14.** Posy is finished. The underside of the flap, marked with a circle, is sticky and can be used to attach your Posy to any suitable flat surface.

# Shaggy Dog

## DESIGNED BY DAVID MITCHELL

Shaggy Dog is a two-piece design—the body and tail are made from one note and the head from another. The body is just about as basic as a body can get. You may need to stretch your imagination slightly to see that the dog has a shaggy coat and that its legs are completely concealed by long hair, which would drag along the ground. The head is only a little more detailed, just a pair of rectangular ears and a slanted nose, but somehow these elements, in combination, are sufficient to suggest a definite shaggy doggyness.

**Requirements:** Shaggy Dog is made from two 3" (76mm) square notes. Ideally both notes should be the same color. The design will work using rectangular notes, though the proportions of the body, ears, and nose will change.

**1.**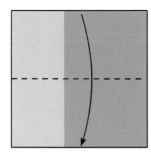

**3.**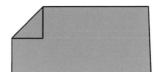

**2.**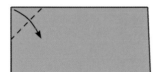

**4.**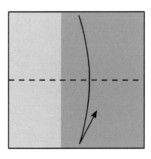

### FOLDING THE BODY

Begin with a 3″ (76mm) square note of any suitable color arranged in the way shown in picture 1, so that the adhesive strip is visible.

**1.** Fold in half from top to bottom. The adhesive strip will stick to itself. Make sure the edges of the two layers of paper lie on top of each other as neatly as possible.

**2.** Form the tail with this small diagonal fold.

**3.** Shaggy Dog's body is finished.

### FOLDING THE HEAD

Begin with a second 3″ (76mm) square note of the same color arranged in the way shown in picture 4, so that the adhesive strip is visible.

**4.** Fold in half from top to bottom, crease firmly, then unfold.

**5.**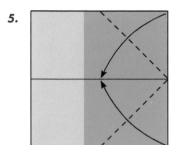

**7.**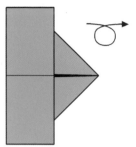

**9.**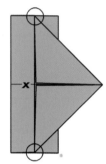

**6.**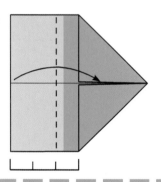

**8.**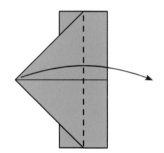

**5.** Use the crease made in step 4 as a guide to help you make these folds.

**6.** Fold approximately two thirds of the rectangular area of paper across to the right, as shown. Picture 7 shows what the result should look like.

**7.** Turn over sideways.

**8.** Fold the triangular flap across to the right.

**9.** Press on the points marked with circles to stick the layers firmly together at the top and bottom of the model. Make sure the layers in the center of the model at point **x** are not stuck together.

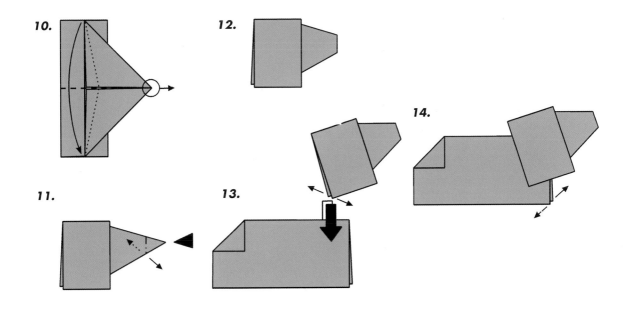

**10.** With these preparations complete, simultaneously pull gently on the point of the nose (marked with a circle) and fold the head in half from top to bottom. The result of this should be the formation of a new crease in the middle layer of paper along the line of the dotted line, which makes the nose point downward. This may take you several attempts to get right. Look at picture 11 to see the result.

**11.** Open up the layers of the nose and push the pointed tip inside out between them. Look at picture 12 to see what the result should look like.

**12.** Shaggy Dog's head is finished.

### ASSEMBLING SHAGGY DOG

**13.** Separate the layers at the bottom of the ears and slide the head down over the body. Press the layers back together to secure the head in place.

**14.** Finally separate the layers at the front of the body slightly so that Shaggy Dog will stand.

# My Cheating Heart

DESIGNED BY OLIVER ZACHARY

My Cheating Heart is not named for the song or its appropriateness to any romantic situation, but for the small cut that makes the design possible. To many paperfolders cutting into origami designs is a form of cheating, but to others it is an integral part of paper-folding techniques. Many traditional Japanese designs rely on cuts for their effect.

When My Cheating Heart is finished you can use the exposed part of the adhesive strip on the back to attach it to any suitable flat surface. You could even attach it to a larger sticky note, as a decoration to an existing message. This is an obvious choice for Valentine's Day.

**Requirements:** My Cheating Heart is folded from a 1.5" x 2" (38mm x 51mm) note. The obvious color choice is pink or red, but you may wish to be a little more creative than this.

**1.**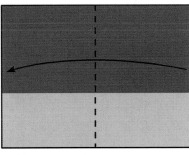

**2.**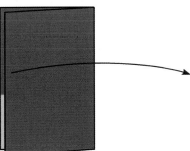

**3.**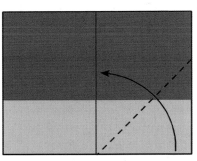

**4.**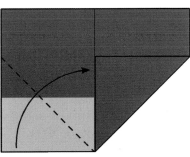

Begin with a 1.5" x 2" (38mm x 51mm) note of any suitable color arranged in the way shown in picture 1, so that the adhesive strip is visible.

**1.** Fold in half from right to left. Crease firmly.

**2.** Open out the fold made in step 1.

**3.** Fold the lower right-hand corner over so that the right-hand half of the bottom edge lies along the crease you made in step 1.

**4.** Fold the lower left-hand corner over in a similar way.

**5.**

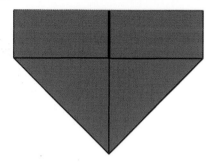

**7.**

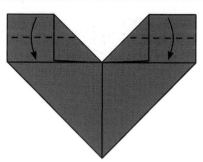

**6.**

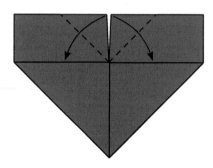

**8.**

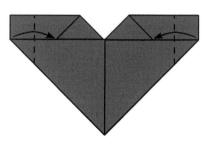

**5.** Cut along the thick black line. Make sure you only cut down as far as the top edges of the triangular flaps.

**6.** Fold the two new corners created by the cut, so that they lie along the top edges of the triangular flaps below them.

**7.** Fold both top edges down to lie along the edges of the triangular flaps below them.

**8.** Fold the outside edges inward in the way shown here. Look at picture 9 to see the result.

**9.**

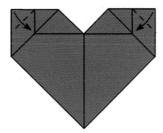

**11.**

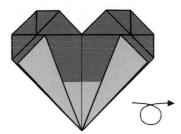

**10.**

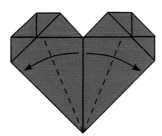

**12.**

**9.** Make these two tiny folds to get rid of the last two square corners and complete the "rounded" outline of the heart. Crease really firmly.

**10.** If you want to be able to attach My Cheating Heart to a suitable flat surface, make these two extra folds to uncover part of the adhesive strip.

**11.** Turn over sideways.

**12.** My Cheating Heart is finished.

# Oblong Carp

DESIGNED BY OLIVER ZACHARY

The best thing about trying to design an origami fish is that it doesn't particularly matter what the design looks like. As long as it has a recognisable tail and a pointed body of some sort it should start to resemble a fish. But despite this, fish designs tend not to be particularly simple. The tail is often complicated to fold, and then there are the fins. This design overcomes the problem with the help of a couple of small cuts. The result is the Oblong Carp. We are used to seeing fish in cans, but in this case there appears to be a can inside the fish!

When the Oblong Carp is finished you can use the exposed part of the adhesive to attach it to any suitable flat surface. Oblong Carp swim best in schools.

**Requirements:** You will need one 1.5" x 2" (38mm x 51mm) note of any color for each Oblong Carp. With slight adjustments, the design will work from many other rectangles as well.

**1.**

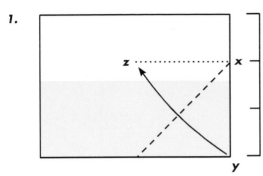

**2.**

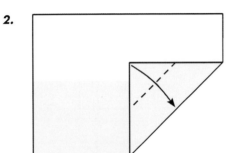

**3.**

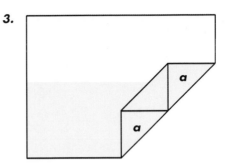

**4.**

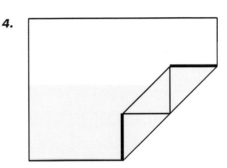

Begin with a 1.5" x 2" (38mm x 51mm) note arranged in the way shown in picture 1, so that the adhesive strip is visible.

**1.** Fold the bottom right-hand corner over so that point **y** ends up at **z**. Edge **xy** will then be lying along the imaginary line **xz**, which is parallel to the top edge of the note. Point **x** is roughly two-thirds of the way up the right-hand edge. This sounds more complicated than it is. Look at picture 2 to see what the result should look like.

**2.** Make this fold so that the result looks as much as possible like picture 3, but do not crease it firmly yet.

**3.** Adjust your fold so that the two small triangular areas marked **a** are the same size and shape. Crease firmly.

**4.** Release the tail by cutting two small slits along the thick black lines.

**5.**

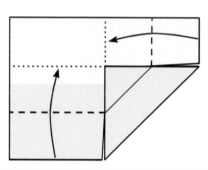

**7.**

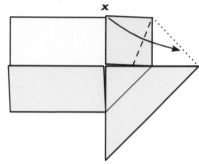

**6.**

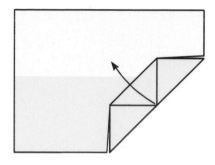

**8.**

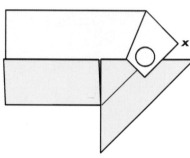

**5.** Open out the fold made in step 2.

**6.** Fold the remainder of the original bottom and right-hand edges over as shown, so that they line up with the edges of the triangular flap.

**7.** Form the dorsal fin by folding point **x** onto an imaginary line drawn between the top right-hand corner of the model and the tip of the tail.

**8.** Tuck the flap marked with a circle underneath the flap immediately below it.

**9.**

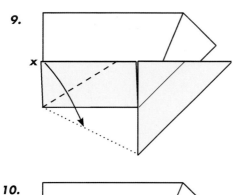

**10.**

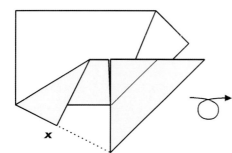

**11.**

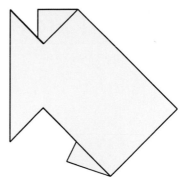

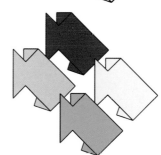

**9.** Form the lower fin by folding point **x** onto an imaginary line drawn between the bottom left-hand corner of the model and the tip of the tail.

**10.** The Oblong Carp is finished. Turn over and rotate into the correct position.

**11.** The Oblong Carp can be varied by changing the size of the tail in step 1.

# Basketball Hoop

ADAPTED FOR STICKY NOTES
BY DAVID MITCHELL

This is a simplified version of a playground fold from the USA. The fold is almost certainly modern rather than traditional, but nobody now seems to remember who invented it or which town or city it came from. Sometimes paperfolds like this just appear out of thin air. Very occasionally they become classics like this one.

The original fold came complete with a stand, but when folding the Basketball Hoop from a sticky note the stand is unnecessary since the hoop can be stuck directly onto any suitable flat surface.

Balls to aim at the Basketball Hoop can easily be made by screwing up tiny pieces of scrap paper.

**Requirements:** The Basketball Hoop is best made from a single 3" (76mm) square note of any color. You will also need some scraps of paper to screw up into balls.

**1.**

**2.**

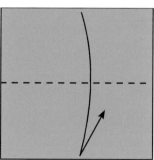

**3.**

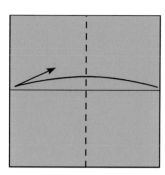

**4.**

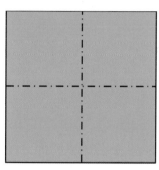

Begin with a 3" (76mm) square note arranged in the way shown in picture 1, so that the adhesive strip is not visible.

**1.** The dotted line marks the position of the edge of the adhesive strip.

**2.** Fold in half from top to bottom, crease firmly, then unfold.

**3.** Fold in half from right to left, crease firmly, then unfold.

**4.** Pick the note up and gently reverse the direction of the creases made in steps 1 and 3, without letting the note stick to itself at any point.

**5.**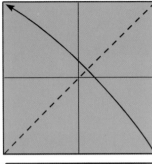

**7.**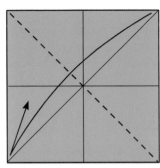

**6.**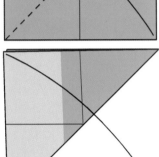

**8.**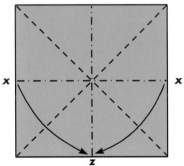

**5.** Check that the adhesive strip is still in the position shown in picture 1. Fold the square in half diagonally, as shown.

**6.** Open out the fold made in step 5.

**7.** Fold in half diagonally in the other direction, crease firmly, then unfold.

**8.** Fold points **x** and **y** onto point **z**. Make both folds at the same time, using only the existing creases. If you have followed steps 1 through 7 correctly the paper will automatically collapse into the shape shown in picture 9 as you do this.

**9.**

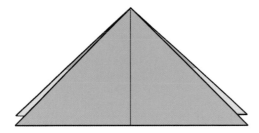

**10.**

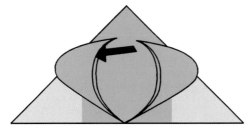

**11.**

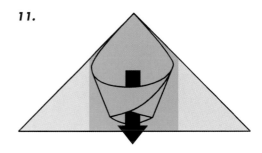

**9.** Make sure all the folds lie flat. To form the hoop curl the front flaps upward and inward in the way shown in picture 10.

**10.** Insert the tip of one flap inside the other to form the hoop. Slide the two flaps into each other until they are securely locked. There should be a small hole in the bottom of the hoop.

**11.** The Basketball Hoop is finished. Attach to any suitable upright surface, such as a wall, partition, or VDU screen, and bombard with tiny balls made from screwed up paper.

# Fred

## DESIGNED BY DAVID MITCHELL

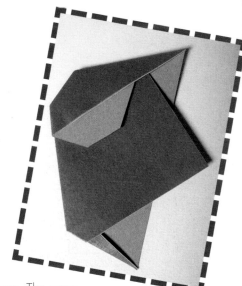

Fred is a minimalist design in a style of origami that is sometimes known as "drawing with paper." In this style simple pictures are created by using the contrast between the two sides of a sheet of paper (which have to be easy to distinguish from each other visually). Designs of this kind are usually folded from a single sheet of paper that has been left white on one side and overprinted with a single plain color on the other. Most commercial origami paper is of this type. The same effect can be created using sticky notes by making a compound square out of two notes of contrasting colors attached back to back. The extra thickness of the paper means that the designs must be extremely simple.

**Requirements:** Fred is made from a compound square formed by attaching two 3" (76mm) square notes back to back. You should use two notes of distinctly different colors, one of which will form Fred's hat and face and the other his mouth and eyes.

**1.**

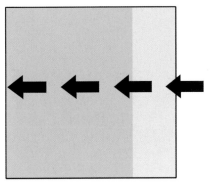 

**2.**

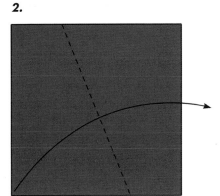

### CREATING A COMPOUND SQUARE

Begin with two 3″ (76mm) square notes of any two suitable colors arranged in the way shown in picture 1.

**1.** Arrange the two notes as shown then lay one on top of the other making sure that all the edges line up exactly. The adhesive strips will seal the left- and right-hand edges completely. The top and bottom edges will be partly open but this will not adversely affect the design.

### FOLDING FRED

Begin with the compound square arranged so that the colour you wish to form Fred's hat and face is visible.

**2.** Make this fold so that the result looks as much as possible like picture 3. Don't crease firmly at this point.

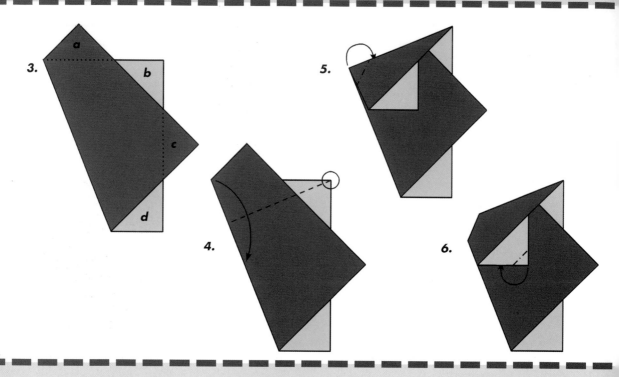

**3.** Adjust your fold until all the small triangular areas marked **a**, **b**, **c** and **d** are the same size and shape. Crease firmly.

**4.** This fold creates the eyes. Note that the crease runs exactly to the corner of the point marked with a circle. Picture 5 shows what the result should look like.

**5.** Tuck the tip of the top left-hand corner away behind to create the outline of Fred's flat cap. Crease really firmly.

**6.** Tuck the tip of this flap inside the layers to round off the eye.

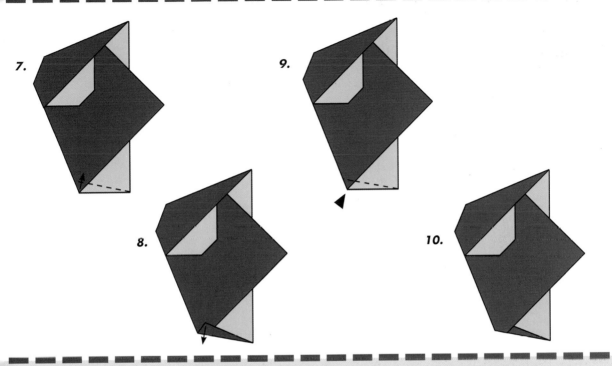

**7.** This tiny fold creates the mouth.

**8.** Open out the fold made in step 7.

**9.** Turn the point inside out between the layers by reversing the direction of the crease made in step 7.

**10.** Fred is finished.

# Alien

## DESIGNED BY DAVID MITCHELL

Alien is a good example of a design that is quickly established by a few accurately located folds, then polished up by a series of finishing folds that can be varied to taste. By step 10 all the elements of the design are in place, the rest is just rounding off and finishing.

The folding sequence also provides a "surprise" finish, since the shaping folds are performed with the face hidden from view. The face is only revealed once the design is turned over. Because of this element of surprise the Alien can be used as a simple performance piece. Tell no one what it is you are folding. Deliberately distract them from seeing the beginnings of the face at step 11 (perhaps by holding it sideways or upside down in relation to the audience), and then, voila, the Alien is revealed!

**Requirements:** Alien is made from a compound square formed by attaching two 3" (76mm) square notes back to back. You should use two notes of distinctly different colors, one of which will form the Alien's skin and the other its mouth and eyes.

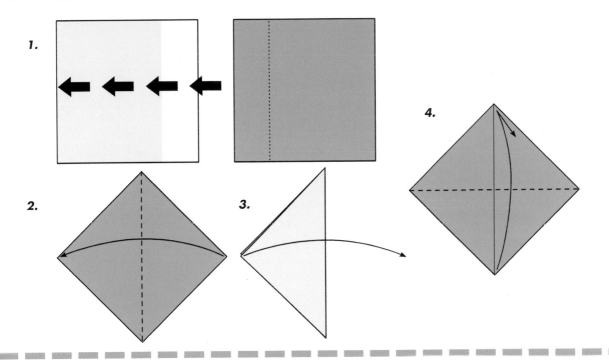

## CREATING A COMPOUND SQUARE

Begin with two 3" (76mm) square notes of any two suitable colors, arranged in the way shown in picture 1.

**1.** Arrange the two notes as shown then lay one on top of the other making sure that all the edges line up exactly. The adhesive strips will seal the left- and right-hand edges completely. The top and bottom edges will be partly open but this will not adversely affect the design.

## FOLDING ALIEN

Begin with the compound square arranged in the way shown in picture 2, so that the color you wish to form the Alien's skin is visible.

**2.** Fold in half diagonally from right to left. Crease firmly.

**3.** Open out the fold made in step 2.

**4.** Fold in half diagonally, from bottom to top, crease firmly, then unfold.

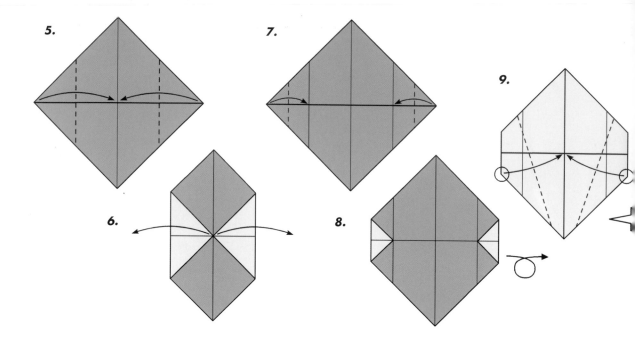

**5.** Fold the right- and left-hand corners into the center, as shown.

**6.** Open out the folds made in step 5.

**7.** Fold the right- and left-hand corners in to the quarter way points, as shown.

**8.** This is the result. Turn over sideways.

**9.** Fold the two corners marked with circles into the exact center of the model. The next picture is drawn to a larger scale.

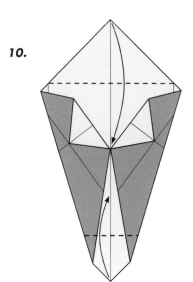

**10.**

**11.**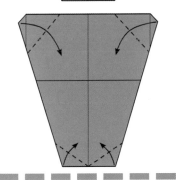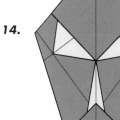

**12.**

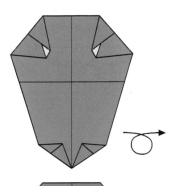

**13.**

**14.**

**10.** Fold the top point down to the exact center of the model and the lower point up to the position shown. Picture 11 shows what the result should look like.

**11.** Turn over sideways.

**12.** Shape the Alien's face by making these four tiny folds. Crease really firmly.

**13.** This is the result. Turn over sideways.

**14.** The Alien is finished.

# Merlin

## DESIGNED BY OLIVER ZACHARY

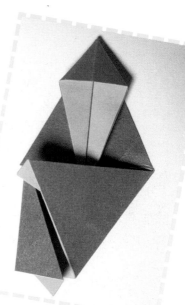

Like Fred and the Alien, Merlin is a design in the minimalist
"drawing with paper" style. The folds do no more than sketch
in the outline details of a tall, robed, and bearded figure,
yet somehow it is enough to suggest the mysterious power
of this legendary enchanter.

In contrast to more traditional designs, with their tight
geometrical precision, some modern designs require that
the folder should locate a crucial fold by eye alone.
Such folds are known as judgement or "right about
there" folds. The slightly skew geometry of Merlin is
entirely based on a fold of this kind (made in step 5). It may take you
several attempts to get the placement of this fold exactly right, but the result will be
worth the effort in the end.

**Requirements:** Merlin is folded from a compound square formed by attaching two 3"
(76mm) square notes back to back. You should use two notes of distinctly different
colors, one of which will form Merlin's robes and the other his face, beard, and hands.

**1.**

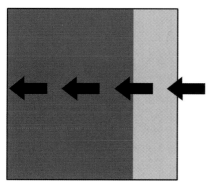 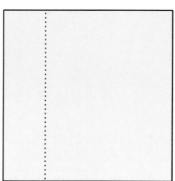

**2.**

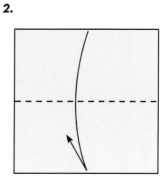

### CREATING A COMPOUND SQUARE

Begin with two 3" (76mm) square notes of any two suitable colors arranged in the way shown in picture 1.

**1.** Arrange the two notes as shown then lay one on top of the other, making sure that all the edges line up exactly. The adhesive strips will seal the left- and right-hand edges completely. The top and bottom edges will be partly open but this will not adversely affect the design.

### FOLDING MERLIN

Begin with the compound square arranged in the way shown in picture 2, so that the color you wish to form Merlin's hands and beard with is visible.

**2.** Fold the paper in half from top to bottom, crease firmly, then unfold.

**3.**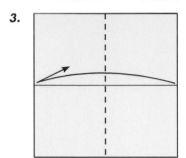

**4.**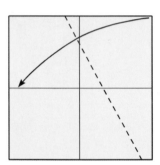

**5.**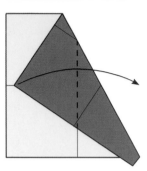

**6.**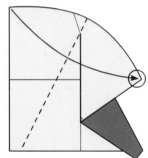

**7.**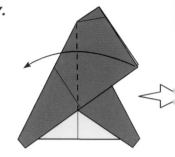

**8.**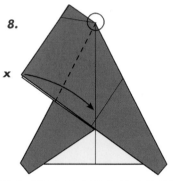

**3.** Fold the paper in half from right to left, crease firmly, then unfold.

**4.** Locate this fold by laying the top right-hand corner onto the horizontal crease, just a little short of the left-hand edge. Look at picture 5 to see what the result should look like.

**5.** Make this fold along the line of the crease made in step 3. Crease firmly but don't try to flatten the rest of the paper. Picture 6 shows what the result should look like.

**6.** This fold is a mirror image of fold 4. You can locate it by folding the top left-hand corner onto the point marked with a

circle. The model will flatten as you crease the fold.

**7.** Fold both layers across to the left, along the line of the vertical crease made in step 3. This fold is similar to the fold made in step 5.

**8.** Fold both layers across to the right making sure that point **x**

**9.**

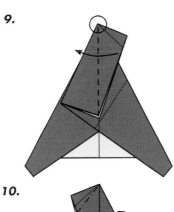

**11.**

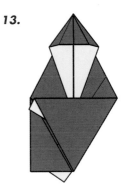

**13.**

**10.**

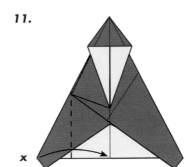

**12.**

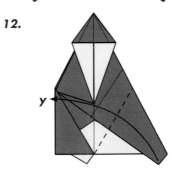

ends up on the vertical crease. Note that the new crease intersects the vertical crease at the point marked with a circle.

**9.** This is the result. Make sure the point at the top of the model is still sharp. Fold both layers across to the left, along the line of the vertical crease made in step 3.

**10.** Fold just the top layer of paper back across to the right and flatten symmetrically to form Merlin's hood, face and beard.

**11.** Fold point **x** onto the vertical center crease to create one arm and hand.

**12.** Make this fold so that **x** ends up at **y**. This fold creates the second arm and hand. Picture

13 shows what the result should look like.

**13.** Merlin is finished. The natural spring in the creases will allow Merlin's hat and robes to loosen so that the model becomes slightly three-dimensional.

# Paradox Cubes

## DESIGNED BY DAVID MITCHELL

Paradox Cubes are paradoxical pictures created by combining simple diamond-shaped tiles. This simple tile is incredibly versatile and can be used to create many different patterns, visual illusions, and impossible figures.

Three tiles can be combined to create a picture of a Paradox Cube, a visual illusion that can be seen either as a solid cube or as a hollow cube—depending on how you look at it. By combining and overlapping Paradox Cubes you can produce a fascinating array of images. Overlapping the edges in different ways, without altering the position of the cubes themselves, changes the perceived spatial relationship of the cubes in a quite bewildering way.

All this is made possible because the adhesive strip is exposed on the back of the tile, so that the tiles can easily be stuck onto a suitable flat surface. This allows you to build the images up in successive overlapping layers.

**Requirements:** Each tile is made from a single 3″ (76mm) square note. Many attractive designs and patterns can be produced by combining tiles folded from notes of three contrasting but complementary colors.

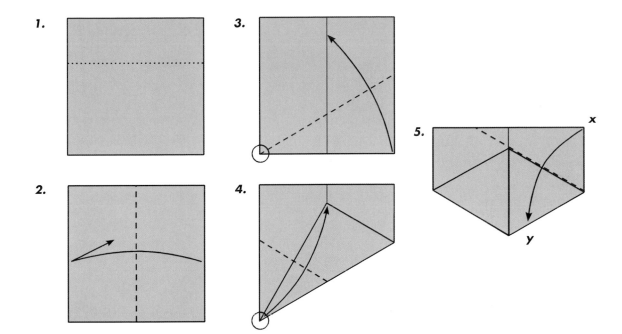

## FOLDING THE TILE

Begin with a 3" (76mm) square note arranged in the way shown in picture 1, so that the adhesive strip is not visible.

**1.** The dotted line marks the position of the edge of the adhesive strip.

**2.** Fold in half from right to left, crease firmly, then unfold.

**3.** Fold the bottom right-hand corner across so that it lies on the vertical crease made in step 2, making sure that the new crease passes exactly through the lower left-hand corner of the paper. Picture 4 shows what the result should look like.

**4.** Fold the bottom left-hand corner over in a similar way. When you have done this the original bottom right and left corners of the paper should lie exactly on top of each other.

**5.** Fold the top right-hand corner marked **x** inward so that it lies on the sloping edge at **y**.

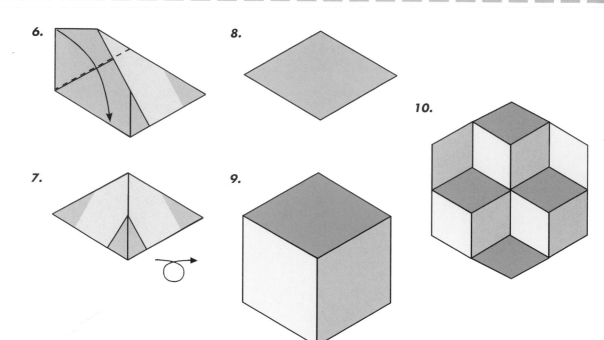

**6.** Fold the top left-hand corner inward in a similar way.

**7.** This is the back of the tile. Turn over sideways.

**8.** The incredibly simple yet versatile Paradox Cube tile is finished. The adhesive strip is exposed on the back of the tile to allow you to attach it to any suitable flat surface. By combining tiles folded from notes of several different colors you can create many interesting patterns, visual illusions and impossible objects.

**9.** Three tiles can be combined to create a simple picture of a cube. This picture is a visual paradox. You can choose to see the center as a corner, which is either pointing toward or away from you. Some people find the alternative image easier to see if the picture is turned upside down.

**10.** You can combine cubes to build up more complex images like this. Given a little practice you can choose to see this picture in two entirely different ways.

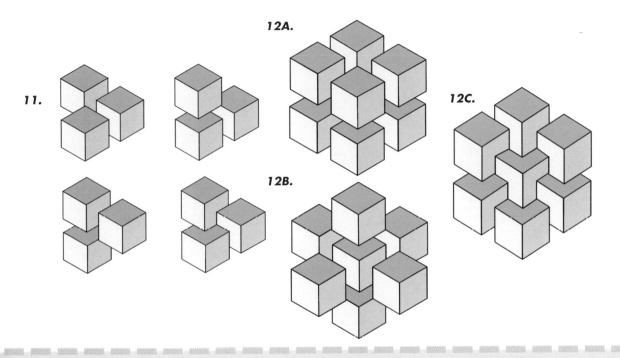

**11.** By overlapping the edges of the cubes in the way shown here, you can produce a bewildering array of images. In each of these pictures the tiles are in exactly the same position. It is only the way in which the edges overlap each other that has been altered.

**12.** The situation becomes even more interesting (and confusing) as the number of cubes increases. Here are just three of the many possible pictures that can be created using seven cubes arranged in a hexagonal pattern. In all of the pictures the twenty-one tiles used are facing the same direction. In **12A** the cubes are arranged to form a larger cube, in **12B** they are arranged to form a cross, while **12C** resembles Escher's famous impossible figure drawings.

# Cairo Tessellation

## DESIGNED BY DAVID MITCHELL

The Cairo Tessellation is an attractive and intriguing pattern of tiles named as a result of its frequent occurrence on the streets of Cairo and in other Islamic centers and sites.

Cairo tiles are a special kind of pentagon that, unlike ordinary regular pentagons, will fit together without leaving gaps between them. Four of these slightly squashed pentagonal tiles will form a stretched hexagon. In the final pattern, stretched hexagons laid in a vertical direction intersect other stretched hexagons laid horizontally across and through them. If you make the tiles in four different colors the resulting pattern is particularly interesting and attractive.

**Requirements:** Each tile is made from a single 3" (76mm) square note. An attractive tessellation can be made by combining tiles folded from notes of four contrasting but complementary colors.

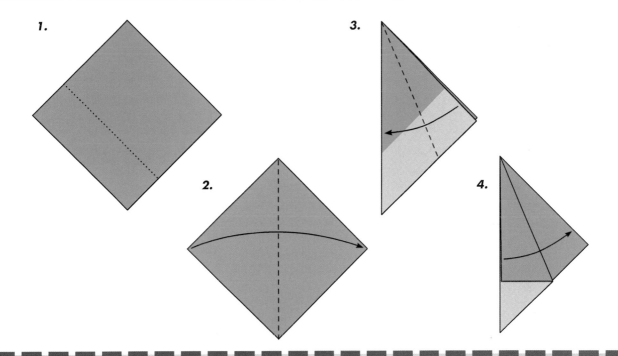

**FOLDING THE CAIRO TILE**

Begin with a 3" (76mm) square note arranged in the way shown in picture 1, so that the adhesive strip is not visible.

**1.** The dotted line marks the position of the edge of the adhesive strip.

**2.** Fold in half diagonally from left to right.

**3.** Make this fold in just the top layer. The crease created by this fold is not used in the final design but is required in order to locate step 5.

**4.** Open out the fold made in step 3.

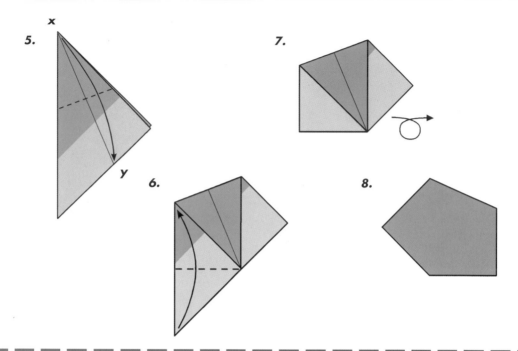

**5.** Fold point **x** onto point **y**. Picture 6 shows what the result should look like.

**6.** Make this fold to complete the outline of the tile.

**7.** This is the back of the tile. Once you have turned it over you will be able to use the exposed areas of the adhesive strip to attach the tiles to any suitable flat surface. Turn over sideways.

**8.** The Cairo tile is finished. Cairo tiles are a special kind of pentagon that will fit together to make an unusual tessellation. At this stage you might like to make several tiles for yourself and try to work out how they fit together. If you make the tiles in four different colors the resulting pattern is particularly attractive.

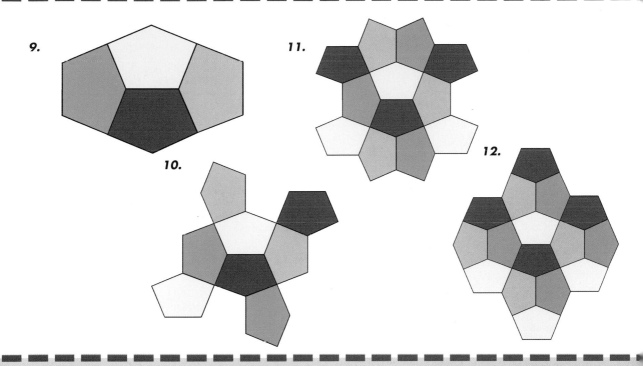

**9.**

**10.**

**11.**

**12.**

### HOW TO CREATE THE CAIRO TESSELLATION

**9.** Four tiles will fit together like this to form a stretched hexagon.

**10.** You can add another four tiles to the edges of the stretched hexagon like this. You will see that all the tiles of the same color are aligned in the same direction.

**11.** The pattern becomes clearer as you add the next four tiles.

**12.** And clearer still when you add four more. You can now see that the original horizontal stretched hexagon has been completely surrounded by vertical stretched hexagons. The surprising nature of the Cairo Tessellation is revealed. You can, of course, keep on adding tiles to this pattern ad infinitum. All you need to remember is that tiles of the same color should always be aligned in the same direction.

# Shooting Stars

## DESIGNED BY DAVID MITCHELL

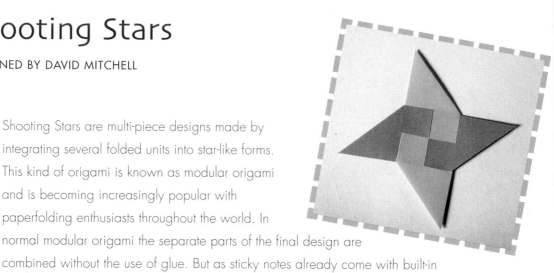

Shooting Stars are multi-piece designs made by integrating several folded units into star-like forms. This kind of origami is known as modular origami and is becoming increasingly popular with paperfolding enthusiasts throughout the world. In normal modular origami the separate parts of the final design are combined without the use of glue. But as sticky notes already come with built-in adhesive strips, you aren't, technically, cheating!

The Single Shooting Star is made from four modules. It makes an attractive decoration but will also fly if thrown from the hand with a flicking motion. Just be careful where you aim it as its edges can be quite sharp.

The Double Shooting Star is made by altering the angle at which the modules are attached to each other from 90 to 45 degrees. As a result the number of modules required for the design doubles to eight.

**Requirements:** You will need four 1.5" x 2" (38mm x 51mm) notes for the Single Shooting Star and eight for the Double Shooting Star. For the best effect you should use two contrasting but complementary colors.

**1.**

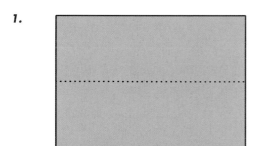

**3.**

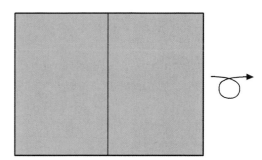

**2.**

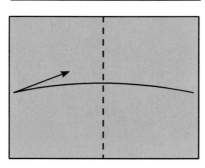

**4.**

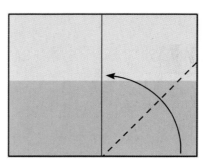

### FOLDING THE MODULES

Begin with a 1.5" x 2" (38mm x 51mm) note of either of your chosen colors arranged in the way shown in picture 1, so that the adhesive strip is not visible.

**1.** The dotted line marks the position of the edge of the adhesive strip.

**2.** Fold in half from right to left, crease firmly, then unfold.

**3.** Turn over sideways.

**4.** Fold the lower right-hand corner over so that the right-hand half of the bottom edge almost, but not quite, lies along the vertical crease you made in step 2.

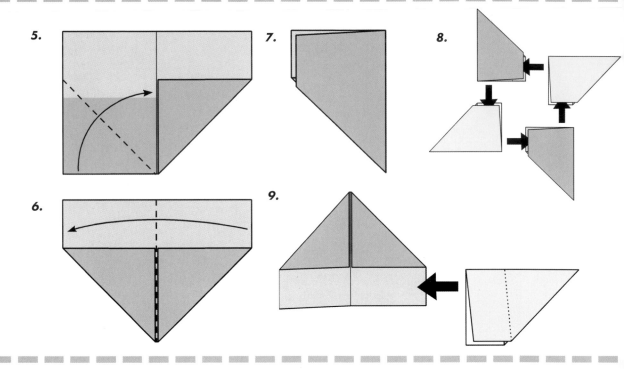

**5.** Fold the lower left-hand corner over in a similar way. You should end up with a slight gap (of about 1mm) between the two edges.

**6.** This is the result. Fold in half by reversing the direction of the crease you made in step 2.

**7.** The module is finished. Fold as many modules as you need.

### ASSEMBLING THE SINGLE SHOOTING STAR

You will need four modules to make a Single Shooting Star.

**8.** The modules go together like this. You will find that once they are in place the sticky part of the notes will hold them firmly together.

**9.** The first two modules can be assembled while the host module is in the fully open position like this. The dotted line marks the position of the edge

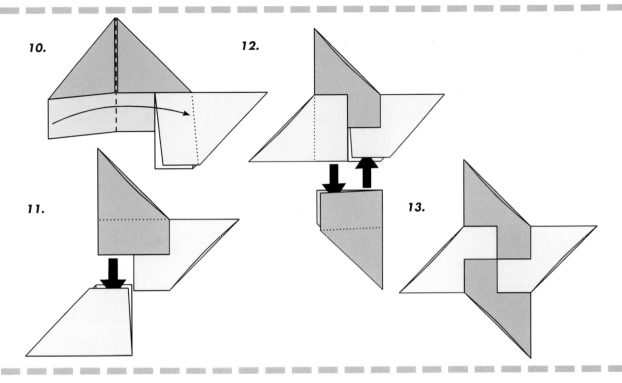

of the hidden flap of paper
inside the module. Picture 10
shows how to use this edge to
align the modules correctly. (Tip:
This edge can clearly be seen if
you hold the modules up to the
light.)  If necessary you will be
able to adjust the position of the
modules in relation to each
other at a later stage.

**10.** Refold the host module to finish
assembling the first two
modules.

**11.** Add the third module to the
assembly like this.

**12.** The fourth module goes outside
the third module but inside the
first.

**13.** When all four modules are
in place the Single Shooting
Star is finished.

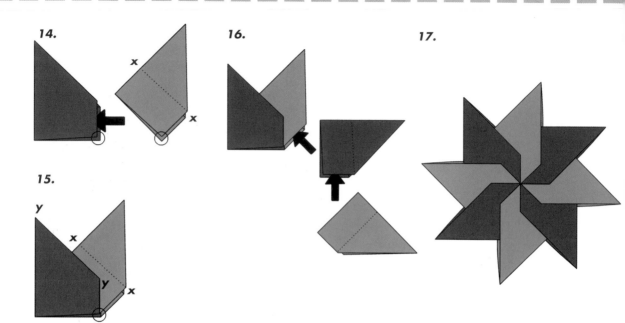

**14.**

**15.**

**16.**

**17.**

### ASSEMBLING THE DOUBLE SHOOTING STAR

You will need eight modules to make a Double Shooting Star.

**14.** The first two modules go together like this. The dotted line **xx** marks the position of the edge of the hidden flap of paper inside the module. Picture 15 shows how to use

this edge to align the modules correctly. (Tip: This edge can clearly be seen if you hold the modules up to the light.) The corners of the modules marked with circles lie on top of each other when the modules are brought together.

**15.** Note that when the modules are correctly assembled edge **yy** on the first module and

hidden edge **xx** on the second module lie parallel to each other. You will find that the sticky strip inside the host module will hold the two modules together.

**16.** Continue to add modules in this way until all eight are in place.

**17.** When all eight modules are in place the Double Shooting Star will look like this.

# Octagon Ring

## DESIGNED BY DAVID MITCHELL

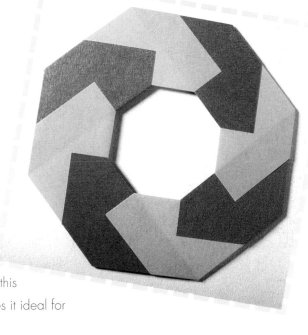

The Octagon Ring is a modular design in the form of an octagonal ring surrounding an octagonal hole. It is made from eight extremely simple modules.

Modular origami rings and stars often conceal hidden patterns, which can be revealed by holding them up to the light. The pattern hidden inside this ring is particularly attractive and makes it ideal for use as a window decoration.

**Requirements:** You will need eight 1.5" x 2" (38mm x 51mm) notes. Ideally you should use two notes in each of two contrasting but complementary colors, or two notes in each of four colors.

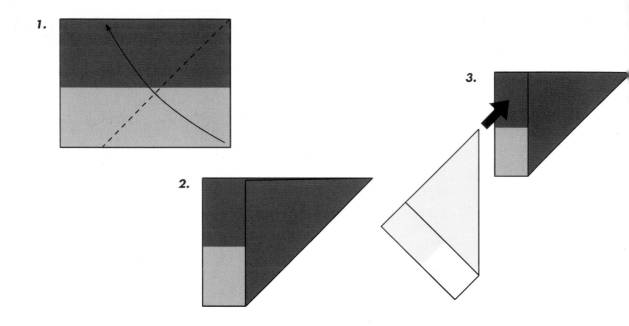

## FOLDING THE MODULES

Begin with a 1.5" x 2" (38mm x 51mm) note of either of your chosen colors arranged in the way shown in picture 1, so that the adhesive strip is visible.

**1.** Fold the right-hand edge onto the top edge and crease firmly.

**2.** Surprisingly, the module is already almost finished. Fold all eight modules to this stage. The next picture is drawn to a smaller scale.

## ASSEMBLING THE OCTAGON RING

**3.** Place the second module on top of the first so that the long edge of the triangular flap on the second module lies along the short edge of the triangular flap on the first. Picture 4 shows what the result should look like.

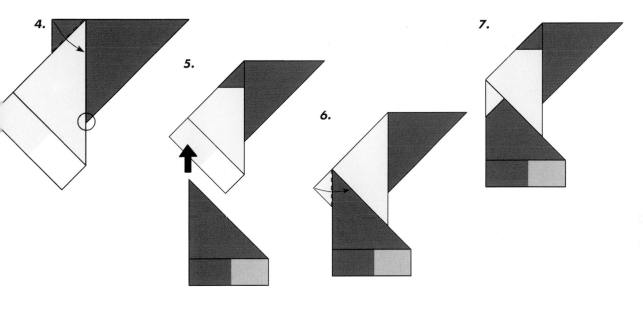

**4.** The modules will be stuck together at the point marked with a circle but will be loose at the top. Make this small fold to hold the modules more firmly together.

**5.** Add a third module by repeating step 3.

**6.** Secure the third module in place by repeating step 4.

**7.** Continue to add and secure modules together by repeating steps 3 and 4 until all eight modules are in place, then link modules one and eight together in a similar way.

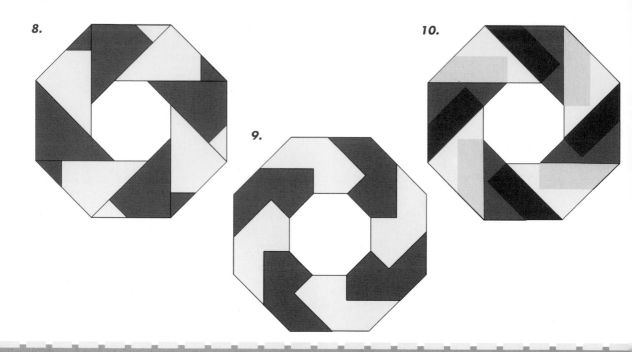

**8.** The assembly process is complete. Turn over to reveal the Octagon Ring.

**9.** This is the finished ring. The Octagon Ring conceals a hidden pattern which can be revealed by holding the ring up to the light. See picture 10.

**10.** Because of this hidden pattern the Octagon Ring is particularly attractive when used to decorate a window.

# Octagon Star

## DESIGNED BY DAVID MITCHELL

The Octagon Star is a modular design in
the form of an eight-pointed star
surrounding an octagonal hole. In
modular origami, it is normal for the
folding of the modules to be
completed before the assembly stage,
but in this particular design the two
stages of module folding and assembly are
intertwined, each of the modules being used as a template for the
next in line.

When finished, the Octagon Star can be used as a decoration but it will also make
an attractive frame to complement a photo of a partner, friend, relative, or pet, or that
blackmail-worthy snapshot from last year's office party.

**Requirements:** You will need eight 1.5" x 2" (38mm x 51mm) notes. For the best
effect you should use four notes in each of two contrasting but complementary colors, or
two notes in each of four colors.

**1.**
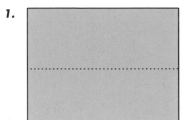

**3.**

**5.**
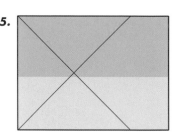

**2.**
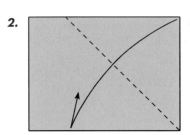

**4.**
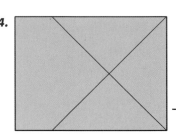

**6.**
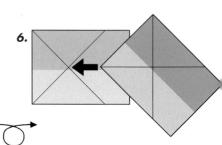

### FOLDING THE MODULES

Begin with a 1.5″ x 2″ (38mm x 51mm) note of one of your chosen colors arranged in the way shown in picture 1, so that the adhesive strip is not visible.

**1.** The dotted line marks the position of the edge of the adhesive strip.

**2.** Fold the right-hand edge onto the bottom edge, crease firmly then unfold.

**3.** Fold the right-hand edge onto the top edge, crease firmly then unfold.

**4.** Turn over sideways.

**5.** The modules are now used as templates for each other. Fold

all the notes to this stage and then follow the instructions below. The next picture is drawn to a smaller scale.

### ASSEMBLING THE OCTAGON STAR

**6.** Attach two notes of different colors together like this, using

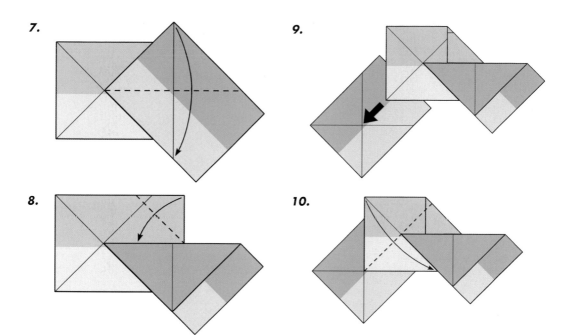

**7.**

**8.**

**9.**

**10.**

the creases made in steps 2
and 3 as a guide.

**7.** Make this fold in just the top
module, using the crease made
in step 2.

**8.** Use the top edge of the upper
module as a guide to help you
locate this fold accurately.

**9.** Attach the two-module assembly
to a third module like this,
bearing your overall color
scheme in mind. This is a
repeat of step 6.

**10.** Make the fold shown using the
crease made in step 2. This fold
is only made in the middle
module of the three. This is a
repeat of step 7.

**11.**

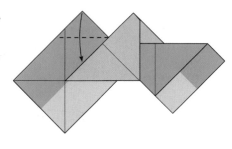

**12.**

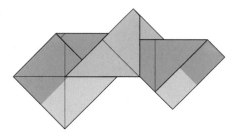

**13.**

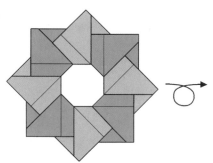

**14.**

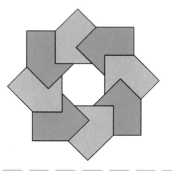

**11.** Repeat step 8 on the lower module.

**12.** Repeat steps 9, 10, and 11 until all eight modules are in place. You will need to lock the first and last modules together in a similar way to complete the star.

**13.** This is the result. Turn over to reveal the Octagon Star.

**14.** The Octagon Star is complete.

# Circle of Squares

DESIGNED BY DAVID MITCHELL

Circle of Squares is a very straightforward design made by combining 32 square sticky notes in a rotational pattern. The notes are combined by means of their adhesive strips, but, because each note is set at an angle to the one below, an area of each strip is left exposed at the back. This will allow you to display the finished Circle of Squares on any flat surface.

In a sense, Circle of Squares is barely an origami design at all, since only the template used to establish the position of the first four notes is folded. But viewed from another perspective, Circle of Squares is a pretty perfect example of the style of paperfolding sometimes known as NOFO or No Fold Origami.

**Requirements:** You will need 32 of the 3″ (76mm) square notes in four contrasting but complementary colors, plus one spare note of the same size but any color to use as the template.

**1.**

**2.**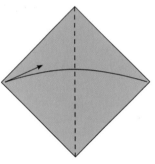

**3.**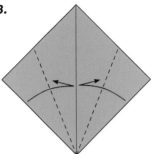

**4.**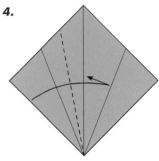

**5.**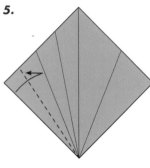

### FOLDING THE TEMPLATE

Begin with a 3" (76mm) square note of any color, arranged in the way shown in picture 1 so that the adhesive strip is not visible.

**1.** The dotted line marks the position of the edge of the adhesive strip.

**2.** Fold in half from right to left, crease firmly, then unfold.

**3.** Fold both the lower edges onto the vertical crease made in step 2, crease firmly, then unfold.

**4.** Fold the lower left edge onto the crease made on the right-hand half of the paper in step 3, crease firmly, then unfold.

**5.** Fold the lower left edge onto the crease made on the left-hand half of the paper in step 3, crease firmly, then unfold.

**6.** The template is finished.

### ASSEMBLING THE CIRCLE OF SQUARES

**7.** Fold in the left-hand edge of the template using the crease made

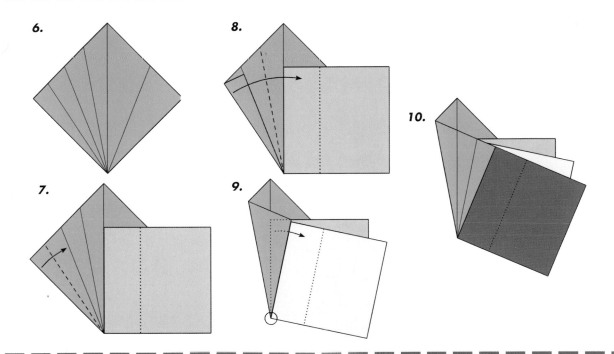

**6.**

**7.**

**8.**

**9.**

**10.**

in step 5, then attach the first square note to the front of the template using the vertical crease made in step 2 as a guide. Make sure this note is arranged in the way shown so that the adhesive strip is not visible. The dotted line marks the position of the edge of the adhesive strip.

**8.** Make this fold in the template using the crease made on the left-hand half of the paper in step 3.

**9.** Attach the second square note to the first using the edge of the template as a guide. Make sure this second note is arranged in the way shown here. It is important to make sure that the corners of all the notes line up

as exactly as possible at the point marked with a circle, which will form the center of the finished design. Once you are happy that the note is in the correct position pull out the hidden flap on the template.

**10.** Attach the third square note to the second using the edge of the template as a guide. Make sure this third note is arranged

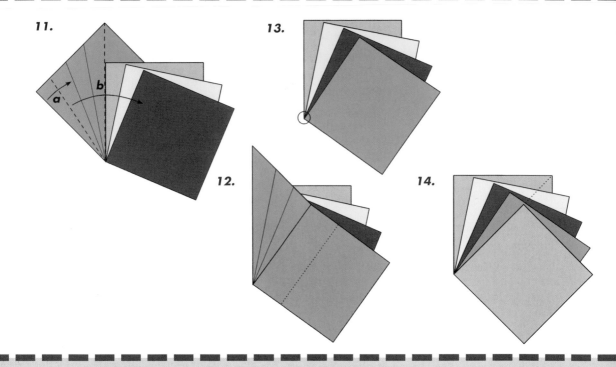

in the way shown here. Once you are happy that this note is in the correct position open out the template to its original position.

**11.** Make fold **a** then fold **b** to reform the template for the last time.

**12.** Attach the fourth square note to the third using the edge of

the template as a guide. Make sure this fourth note is arranged in the way shown here. Once you are happy that this note is in the correct position remove all the notes from the template, being careful not to disturb their relative positions. You will not need the template again.

**13.** Check that the corners of all four notes are accurately

aligned to each other at the point marked with a circle. Adjust slightly if necessary. The remaining 28 notes can be attached one by one using the method explained in step 14.

**14.** This picture shows how to align the edge of the fifth note, the second note of the first color, on an imaginary line drawn between the center of

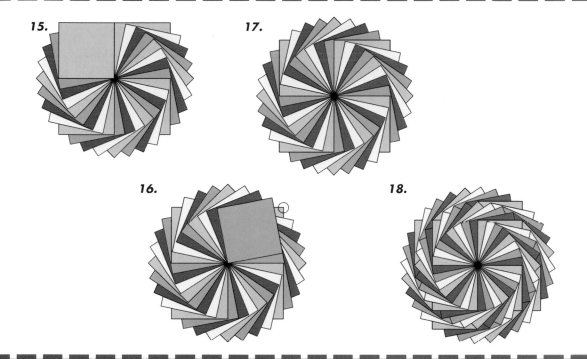

**15.**

**17.**

**16.**

**18.**

the design and the outside corner of the previous note of the same color. All the remaining notes are then added, in strict color sequence.

**15.** When you reach this stage you will be able to check, and if necessary correct, the alignment of your last seven notes with reference to the edges of the first seven.

**16.** All 32 notes are in place. To complete the design tuck the last seven notes underneath the first (the corner of which is marked with a circle on this picture).

**17.** The Circle of Squares is finished. The circle is, of course, an optical illusion. A small portion of the adhesive strip of each note is exposed at the back and can be

used to attach the finished design to any suitable flat surface.

**18.** And if that wasn't enough for you, you might like to work out how to create this 64 note version of the Circle of Squares!

# Spinners

## DESIGNED BY DAVID MITCHELL

Spinners are wonderfully simple origami toys. They were inspired by a hanging ornament designed by the American paperfolder Alice Gray. If you hold a Spinner carefully between the palms of your cupped hands and blow gently at the very top the Spinner will spin rapidly.

Spinners are modular designs. The minimum number of modules required for a Spinner is four. You may like to ascertain a sensible upper figure by experimenting for yourself. The number of modules required will, however, always be even, since Spinners are made from right- and left-handed modules arranged in pairs.

**Requirements:** You will need a minimum of four 3" (76mm) square notes. For the best effect, you should use notes in pairs of contrasting but complementary colors.

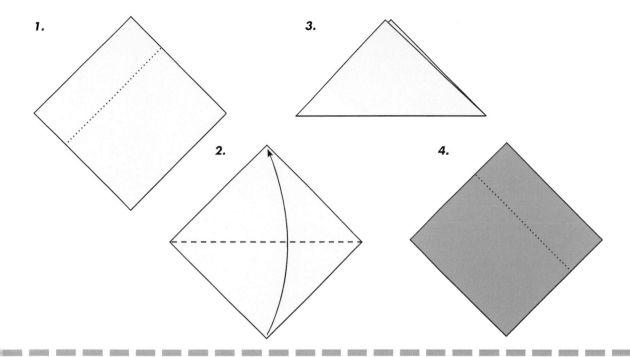

**FOLDING A LEFT-HANDED MODULE**

Begin with a 3" (76mm) square note of one of your chosen colors arranged in the way shown in picture 1, so that the adhesive strip is not visible.

**1.** The dotted line marks the position of the edge of the adhesive strip.

**2.** Fold in half, from bottom to top.

**3.** The left-handed module is finished.

**FOLDING A RIGHT-HANDED MODULE**

Begin with a 3" (76mm) square note of another of your chosen colors arranged in the way shown in picture 4, so that the adhesive strip is not visible.

**4.** The dotted line marks the position of the edge of the adhesive strip.

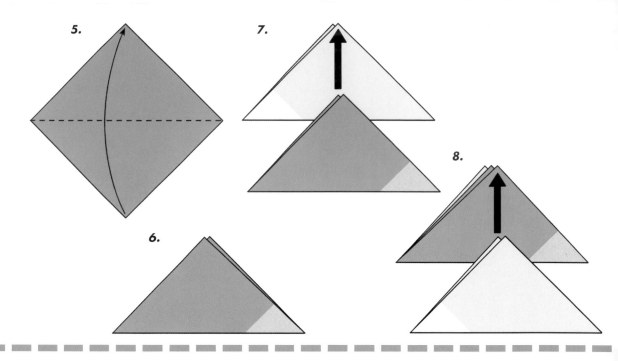

**5.** Fold in half from bottom to top.

**6.** The right-handed module is finished. Make as many modules as you require for your Spinner, in equal numbers of left- and right-handed modules.

### COMBINING THE MODULES

**7.** Attach a right-handed module to the top of a left-handed module, making sure that the edges line up as exactly as possible.

**8.** Add a second left-handed module to the top of the stack.

**9.** Add a second right-handed module to the top of the stack.

**10.** The stack now consists of four modules. You can, if you wish, add further pairs of modules to the stack before you move on to step 11, but it is perhaps best to

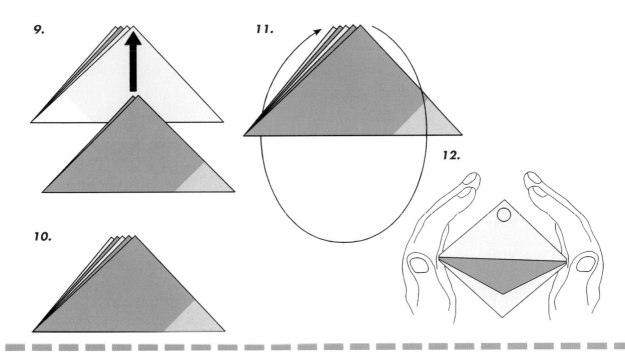

**9.**

**10.**

**11.**

**12.**

make your first Spinner using just these four modules.

**11.** Swing the top layer of the top note forward and downward. Continue the rotation until the note can be stuck to the back of the bottom layer of the bottom note in the stack. Try to line the edges up as exactly as possible.

**12.** The result will be a four-armed Spinner like the one shown here. (The fourth arm is hidden behind the others in the picture.) Arrange the arms as evenly as possible, make sure all the edges are aligned and closed, then hold the Spinner between the palms of your cupped hands and blow gently

at the top of the model (marked with a circle). The Spinner will spin.

Once you have mastered the assembly system you will be able to make Spinners with a larger number of modules.

# Plane

## DESIGNED BY DAVID MITCHELL

The traditional paper dart is one of the most enduring of all origami designs. Every schoolchild knows it. But where did it come from? Who first folded it, and when? Does it predate the invention of real aircraft, or was it designed afterward? We simply do not know.

The traditional dart has wings but no tail. This Plane, however, has both, which gives it added stability for a straight, stall-free flight. Launched in the same way as the traditional paper dart, the Plane will fly remarkably well.

**Requirements:** The Plane is made in three parts from two large and one small rectangular note. Ideally, the two large notes used for the wings should be 3″ x 5″ (76mm x 127mm) and the smaller note used for the tail should be 1.5″ x 2″ (38mm x 51mm). For the best visual effect, the color of the tail should contrast with the wings.

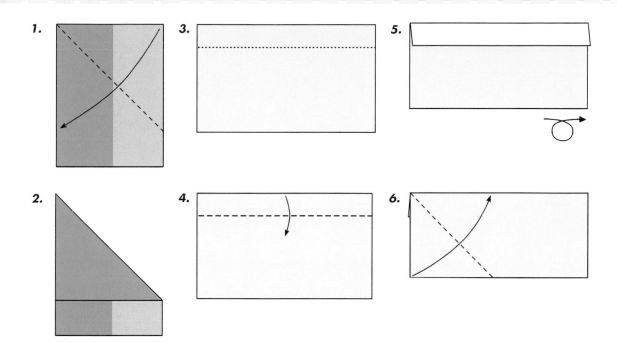

## FOLDING THE TAIL

Begin with a 1.5″ x 2″ (38mm x 51mm) note of the color you have chosen for the tail, arranged in the way shown in picture 1 so that the adhesive strip is visible.

**1.** Fold the top edge onto the left-hand edge and crease firmly.

**2.** The tail is finished.

## FOLDING THE LEFT-HAND WING

Begin with a 3″ x 5″ (76mm x 127mm) note of the color you have chosen for the wings, arranged in the way shown in picture 3 so that the adhesive strip is not visible.

**3.** The dotted line marks the position of the edge of the adhesive strip.

**4.** Fold the adhesive strip into sight.

**5.** Turn over sideways.

**6.** Fold the left-hand edge across to lie along the top edge.

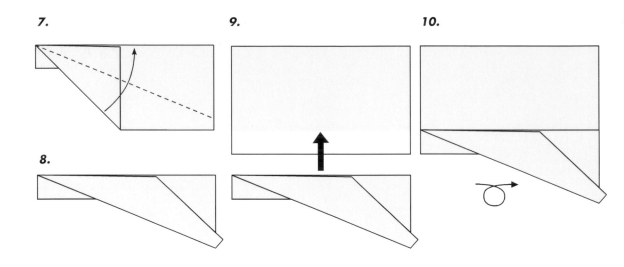

**7.** Fold the sloping edge across to lie along the top edge in a similar way.

**8.** The left-hand wing is finished.

### FOLDING THE RIGHT-HAND WING

Begin with a second 3″ x 5″ (76mm x 127mm) note of the color you have chosen for the wings, arranged in the way shown in picture 9, so that the adhesive strip is visible.

**9.** Attach the left-hand wing to the second note so that the bottom edges and corners line up exactly. Picture 10 shows what the result should look like.

**10.** Turn over sideways.

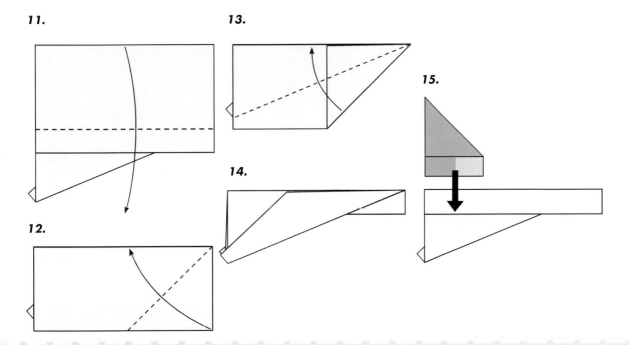

**11.** Make this fold so that the crease lines up exactly with the top of the left-hand wing. The more accurately you do this the better the plane will fly.

**12.** Fold the right-hand edge across to lie along the top edge.

**13.** Fold the sloping edge across to lie along the top edge in a similar way.

**14.** The right-hand wing is finished. Peel the wings gently apart, so that they are completely separate, but make sure to keep the folds made in steps 5 and 11. Now follow steps 15 and 16 to add the tail.

**ADDING THE TAIL**

**15.** Attach the tail to the left-hand wing like this. Picture 16 shows what the result should look like.

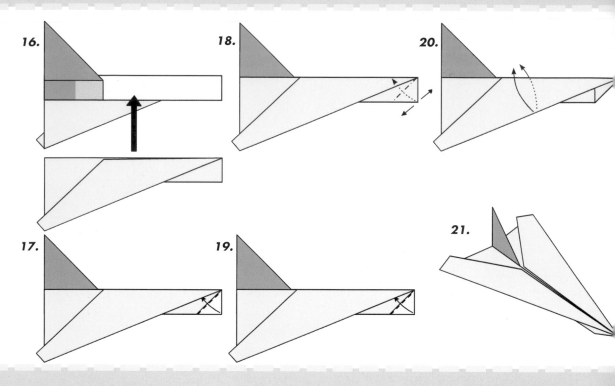

**16.** Re-attach the right-hand wing.

### FORMING THE NOSE

**17.** The Plane will fly well if you go straight to step 20, but to maximize its performance first crease, then unfold, the small fold shown here.

**18.** First peel the layers of the nose carefully apart, then fold the small triangular flap belonging to the top layer away inside, using the crease you made in step 17. After you have made the fold, allow the other layers to stick together again.

**19.** Fold the small triangular flap belonging to the lower layer of the nose around to the front. Make sure it goes underneath the wing before you stick it down, otherwise step 20 will prove impossible.

**20.** Lift the wings so that they are slightly above the level of the fuselage and a slight angle is formed between them.

**21.** The Plane is finished. Launched in the same way as the traditional paper dart, the Plane will fly remarkably well.

# Flexatron

DESIGN ADAPTED FOR STICKY NOTES
BY DAVID MITCHELL

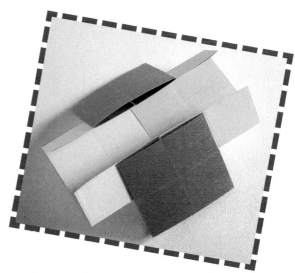

Flexatrons are fascinating flexible toys that change shape and pattern as they are flexed. They are used as advertising handouts, given away in cereal packets, and marketed as children's toys. But now you can make one for yourself, from just four square sticky notes.

When finished the Flexatron will flex and even change color, if you rotate the right and left edges away from you. Rotate the top and bottom edges away from you and it changes shape, from a square to a cross. Flex again and a square reappears, then flex for a fourth and final time and it will return to its original shape and color. You can, of course, continue to flex ad infinitum, or at least until your fingers run out of steam.

**Requirements:** You will need four 3" (76mm) square notes. For the best visual effect, each note should be of a different color.

**1.**

**2.**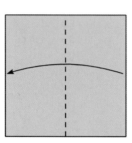

**3.**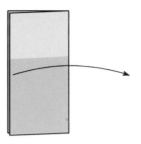

**4.**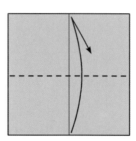

**5.**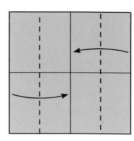

**6.**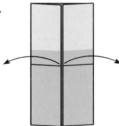

### FOLDING THE MODULES

Begin with a 3" (76mm) square note of one of your four chosen colors arranged in the way shown in picture 1, so that the adhesive strip is not visible.

**1.** The dotted line marks the position of the edge of the adhesive strip.

**2.** Fold in half from right to left.

**3.** Open out the fold made in step 2.

**4.** Fold in half from bottom to top, crease firmly, then unfold.

**5.** Fold the left- and right-hand edges onto the vertical crease made in step 2.

**6.** Open out the folds made in step 5.

**7.** Fold the top and bottom edges onto the horizontal crease made in step 4.

**8.** You have now divided the paper into a grid of 16 small squares. Cut out the two squares marked with circles.

**7.**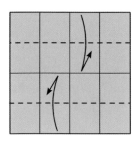

**9.**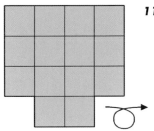

**11.**

**8.**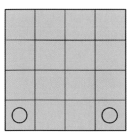

**10.**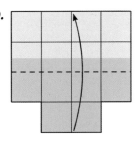

**12.**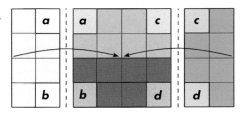

**9.** This is the result. Turn over sideways.

**10.** Fold the lower half of the paper onto the upper half.

**11.** The first module is finished. It will help you when you come to flex the Flexatron if at this stage you make sure that the module will fold forward and backward along each of the horizontal and vertical creases. Make the other three modules.

### ASSEMBLING THE FLEXATRON

**12.** Arrange the four modules like this. The Flexatron is assembled by turning the left- and right-hand modules over on top of the others so that the pairs of small squares marked **aa**, **bb**, **cc**, **dd** end up on top of each other. It is important that each of these pairs of squares is matched up as accurately as possible. Since all of these squares are sticky they will hold together quite firmly on first contact. For this reason you may find it easier to add each piece individually.

**13.**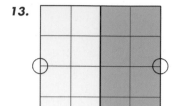

**14.**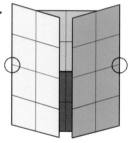

**15.**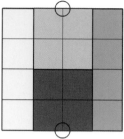

**16.**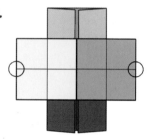

**17.**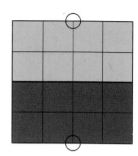

**18.**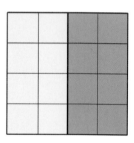

### FLEXING THE FLEXATRON

**13.** The Flexatron is finished. To flex the Flexatron hold it at the points marked with circles and swivel the left- and right-hand edges away from you.

**14.** As you do this the front of the Flexatron will open. Continue swivelling the edges away from you until the points marked with circles meet in the middle at the back.

**15.** The first flex is completed. To flex again hold the Flexatron at the points marked with circles and swivel the top and bottom edges away from you.

**16.** This is the result. To continue flexing hold the Flexatron at the points marked with circles and once again swivel the left- and right-hand edges away from you.

**17.** Now swivel the top and bottom edges away from you again.

**18.** The Flexatron is back in its original state. If you repeat these flexing instructions several times the Flexatron will begin to move much more smoothly.

# Simple Structures

DESIGNED BY TUNG KEN LAM

Each of the three Simple Structures explained in this project is made from three very basic modules, two of which require only one fold.

3L is a sticky note origami version of one of the most famous forms of modular origami, which was invented by the American paperfolder Ed Sullivan. He named the original form XYZ after the three axes of three-dimensional space, which are represented by the three planes of the design. In 3L (so named because it is made from three L-shaped pieces) only part of each of these planes is present in the design.

Steps is a development of 3L made by adding two more right-angle creases to the module to create a stepped or zigzag effect.

3LO is simply 3L without the corners. O stands for Octahedron.

**Requirements:** You will need three 3" (76mm) square notes for each structure. Ideally you should make each structure from notes of three contrasting but complementary colors.

**3L**

**1.**

**2.**

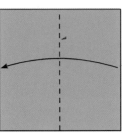

**3.**

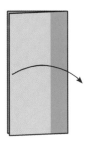

**4.**

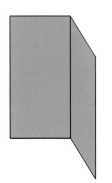

**5.**

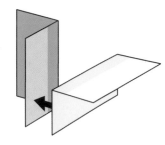

**6.**

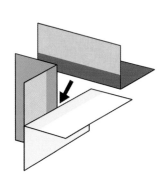

**3L**

Begin with a 3" (76mm) square note in one of your three colors arranged as shown in picture 1, so that the adhesive strip is not visible.

**1.** The dotted line marks the position of the edge of the adhesive strip.

**2.** Fold in half from right to left.

**3.** Open out the fold made in step 2 to an angle of 90 degrees.

**4.** When you have done this the two halves of the paper should stand at right angles to each other. The first module is finished. Fold the other two.

**5.** Put two modules together like this, making sure that the

corners and edges of the modules are aligned along their common boundaries.

**6.** Add the third module like this, making sure you have the adhesive strip in the position shown. Align the corners and edges of all the modules along their common boundaries. You may find you have to allow the

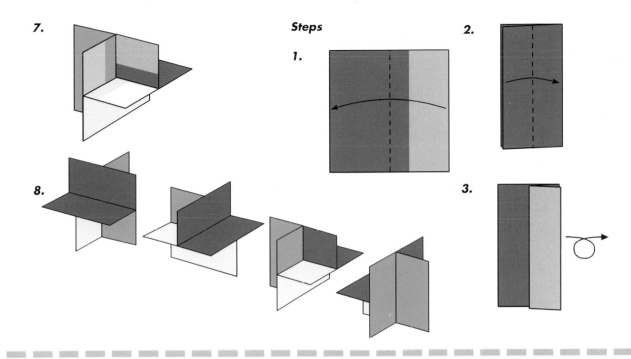

7.

Steps

1.

2.

8.

3.

modules to stick together very slightly out of position at first, then slide them into true alignment. Fortunately the glue on sticky notes will allow you to do this without too much difficulty.

**7.** This is the result. 3L is finished.

**8.** Here are four views of this

strange but fascinating object. In each case 3L has been rotated through 90 degrees around its vertical axis.

**STEPS**

Begin with a 3" (76mm) square note of one of your three colors arranged as shown in picture 1, so that the adhesive strip is visible.

**1.** Fold in half from right to left. You will need to be careful that the paper does not buckle as you flatten this fold.

**2.** Fold just the top flap in half from left to right.

**3.** Turn over sideways.

**4.**

**5.**

**6.**

**7.**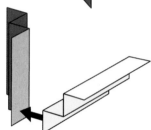

**8.**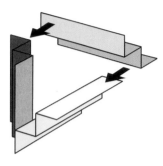

**9.**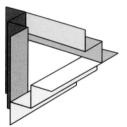

**4.** Fold the top flap in half from right to left.

**5.** Open out the folds made in steps 1, 2, and 4 so that each flap lies at an angle of 90 degrees to its neighbor(s).

**6.** The result should look like this. The first module is finished. Make the other two modules.

**7.** Put two modules together like this. Take care that the adhesive strips on both modules are in the positions shown.

**8.** Add the third module like this, making sure you have the adhesive strip in the position shown. Align the corners and edges of all the modules. Steps is easier to assemble than 3L and you should have no difficulty in getting the modules to stick together in the correct positions.

**9.** This is the result. Steps is finished. This design makes an attractive ornament (although, unlike 3L it will not stand upright in the position shown in these assembly diagrams).

**3LO**

**1.**

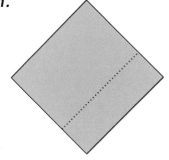

**2.**

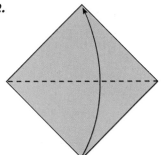

**3.**

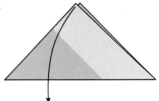

**4.**

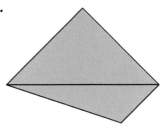

**5.**

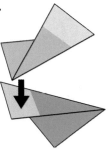

### 3LO

Begin with a 3″ (76mm) square note in one of your three chosen colors arranged as shown in picture 1, so that the adhesive strip is not visible.

**1.** The dotted line marks the position of the edge of the adhesive strip.

**2.** Fold in half diagonally from bottom to top.

**3.** Open out the fold made in step 2 to an angle of 90 degrees.

**4.** When you have done this the two halves of the paper should stand at right angles to each other. The first module is finished. Fold the other two.

**5.** Put two modules together like this, making sure that the corners and edges of the modules are aligned along their common boundaries. Take care that you have the adhesive strips on both modules in the positions shown.

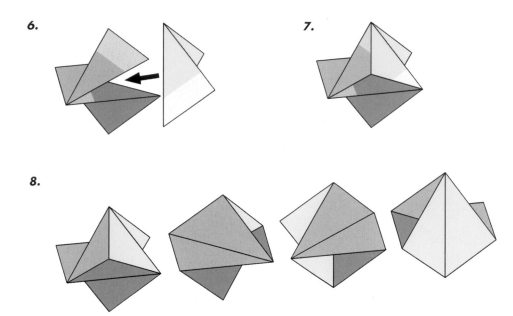

**6.** Add the third module like this, keeping it vertical and making sure you have the adhesive strip in the position shown. Align the corners and edges of all the modules along their common boundaries. You may find you have to allow the modules to stick together very slightly out of position at first, before sliding them into true alignment. Fortunately the glue on sticky notes will allow you to do this without too much difficulty.

**7.** This is the result. 3LO is finished. It will not stand upright in the position shown in these assembly diagrams but will sit quite happily on any of the triangular faces.

**8.** Here are four views of this unique object. In each case 3LO has been rotated through 90 degrees around its vertical axis.

# Roll-up Cube

## DESIGNED BY DAVID MITCHELL

The Roll-up Cube is a modular design assembled as a flat strip, which is then quite literally rolled up to create a three-dimensional structure. Although some sides and angles are obviously missing, it is, nevertheless, indisputably a cube.

One of the most unusual and intriguing aspects of this design is that three of the six modules are mirror images of the other three. This is a property more usually associated with triangular-shaped constructions, so it seems a little odd to encounter it in a cube.

**Requirements:** You will need six 3" (76mm) square notes. For the best effect, you should use two notes in each of three contrasting but complementary colors.

**1.**

**2.**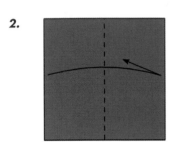

**3.**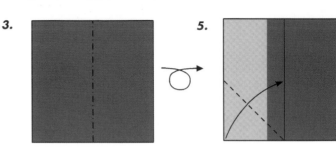

**4.**

**5.**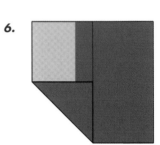

**6.**

## FOLDING THE MODULES

Begin with a 3″ (76mm) square note of one of your colors arranged in the way shown in picture 1, so that the adhesive strip is not visible.

**1.** The dotted line marks the edge of the adhesive strip.

**2.** Fold in half from left to right, crease firmly, then unfold.

**3.** Pick the note up and gently reverse the direction of the horizontal crease, without allowing the note to stick to itself. Turn over sideways.

**4.** Fold all six modules to this stage and divide the modules into two sets. There should be one module of each color in each set. Follow instructions 5 through 7 to fold one set and

instructions 8 through 10 to fold the other.

**5.** Fold the bottom left-hand corner inward using the vertical crease made in step 2 as a guide.

**6.** Make three of these modules in three different colors.

**7.** The first set of modules is finished.

**7.**

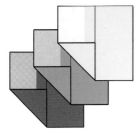

**9.**

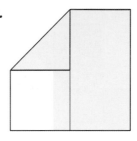

**11.**

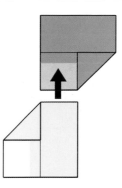

**8.**

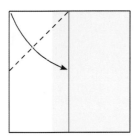

**10.**

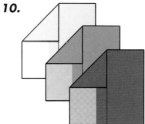

**12.**

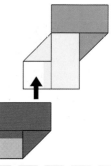

**8.** Starting on the second set, fold the top left-hand corner inward using the vertical crease made in step 2 as a guide.

**9.** Make three of these modules in three different colors.

**10.** The second set of modules is finished.

## ASSEMBLING THE ROLL-UP CUBE

**11.** Select a module of a different color from each set, align them to each other in the way shown here, then attach the second module to the front of the first. Use the left-hand edge of the triangular flap and the left-hand half of the horizontal crease as guides. The exposed adhesive strip on the first module will hold them together.

**12.** Make sure the first two modules are lined up correctly, then add a third. The third module is from the same set as the first module. You should use the module of the third color here. Make sure the third

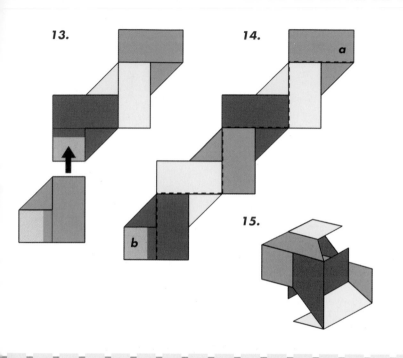

Continue to add modules, alternating modules from the two sets and maintaining the color sequence you have established, until all six modules are in place.

**14.** Check that all the modules are in the correct order and correctly lined up to each other. You will see that the creases made in step 2 have been marked with dashed fold lines. If you pick up both ends of the strip of modules and allow each module to fold at 90 degrees along this existing crease the strip will roll up to form a cube. Press the outside of the module marked **a** against the inside of the module marked **b**. The adhesive strip will hold the two modules together.

**15.** This is the result. The Roll-up Cube is finished.

module is aligned correctly before attaching it to the front of the second. Use the bottom edge of the triangular flap and the lower half of the vertical crease as guides.

**13.** Make sure the second and third modules are lined up correctly, then add a fourth. The

fourth module is from the same set as the second. It should be the same color as the first module you used. Make sure the fourth module is aligned correctly before attaching it to the front of the third. Use the bottom edge of the triangular flap and the lower half of the vertical crease as guides.

# Upsilon

## DESIGNED BY DAVID MITCHELL

Upsilon is one of the pleasant surprises of sticky note origami. The form is that of a kind of "winged-cube," a cube altered by extending each of the faces, in one direction only, by the addition of small triangular flaps. Surprisingly, Upsilon will stand upright on one corner, supported by three of the triangular flaps, which lie flat to the ground. So you could use it as an office ornament to brighten up your desk space.

Like the Roll-up Cube, Upsilon is made from two sets of mirror image modules. You might want to see what happens if you try to make it from six identical ones. (To find this out you'll need to study the method used to fold the module for Spiky Ball—see page 107.)

**Requirements:** You will need six 3" (76mm) square notes. For the best effect you should use two notes in each of three contrasting but complementary colors.

**1.**

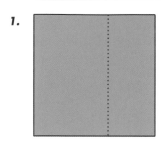

**3.**

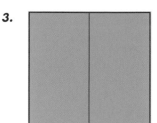

**5.**

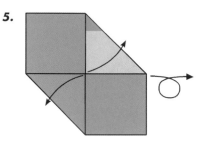

**2.**

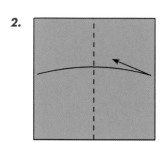

**4.**

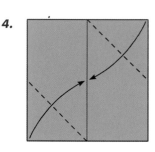

**6.**

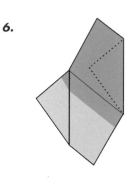

## FOLDING THE MODULES

Begin with a 3" (76mm) square note of one of your chosen colors arranged in the way shown in picture 1, so that the adhesive strip is not visible.

**1.** The dotted line marks the position of the edge of the adhesive strip.

**2.** Fold in half from left to right, crease firmly, then unfold.

**3.** Fold all six modules to this stage. Divide the modules into two sets. There should be one module of each color in each set. Follow instructions 4 through 6 to fold one set and instructions 8 through 10 to fold the other.

**4.** Fold the top right- and bottom left-hand corners inward using the vertical crease made in step 2 as a guide.

**5.** Unfold both triangular flaps through 90 degrees so that they stand up at right angles to the rest of the paper. Turn over and rotate to align to picture 6.

**6.** The finished module should look

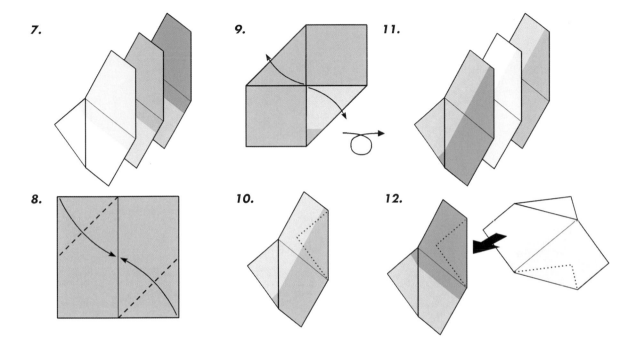

7.

9.

11.

8.

10.

12.

like this. Make three of these modules in three different colors.

**7.** The first set of modules is finished.

**8.** Fold the top left- and bottom right-hand corners inward using the vertical crease made in step 2 as a guide.

**9.** Unfold both triangular flaps

through 90 degrees so that they stand up at right angles to the rest of the paper. Turn over and rotate to align to picture 10.

**10.** The finished module should look like this. Make three of these modules in three different colors.

**11.** The second set of modules is finished.

### ASSEMBLING UPSILON

**12.** Using the first set of modules, attach the first module to the second module like this, making sure that all the corners and edges line up. Make sure that the adhesive strips of both modules are in the positions shown. Picture 13 shows what the result should look like.

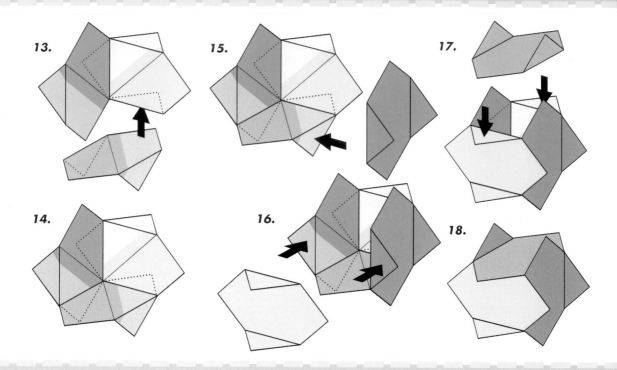

**13.** Attach the third module to the first and second modules like this. Make sure that the adhesive strip is in the position shown and that all the edges of all three modules line up once they are firmly attached together.

**14.** One corner is finished. To complete the design you need to add the other set of modules. *In every case you must*

*remember to attach a flap covered with an adhesive strip to one that is not. If you do this the design will work.*

**15.** Attach the fourth module to the second and third, like this, making sure that all the corners and edges line up. Notice that modules of the same color are added at opposite sides of the design.

**16.** Add the fifth module in the way shown. This time you will need to attach it to three other modules.

**17.** Finally, add the sixth module, like this, making sure that all the corners and edges are aligned.

**18.** Upsilon is finished and will stand upright on one corner.

# Spiky Ball

### DESIGNED BY DAVID MITCHELL

This attractive modular ornament is made up of 18 square faces and eight triangular ones. In this design the triangular faces are missing, which allows light to penetrate inside the structure, and the square faces are surrounded by spiky triangular flaps, which not only link them together but also add visual interest to the exterior of the design.

Spiky Ball is not only the most complex but also the most delicate modular design in this book. Because of its delicate nature you will find that you need to fold the modules from very small squares. A way of creating suitably sized squares, by adapting 3" (76mm) notes, is given at the start of the folding instructions.

**Requirements:** You will need nine 3" (76mm) notes. For the best effect you should use three notes in each of three contrasting but complementary colors.

**1.**

**2.**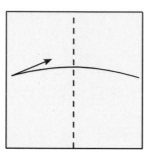

**3.**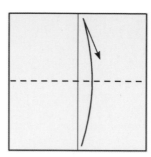

**4.**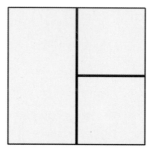

### CREATING SMALLER SQUARES

Begin with a 3" (76mm) square note of one of your chosen colors arranged in the way shown in picture 1.

**1.** The adhesive strip should not be visible.

**2.** Fold in half from right to left, crease firmly, then unfold.

**3.** Fold in half from bottom to top, crease firmly, then unfold.

**4.** Divide the large square into three parts, like this, by cutting along the thick black lines.

**5.** Keep the small squares and dispose of the larger rectangle. You will need 18 small squares for the design. For the best results you should use six squares in each of three contrasting colors.

**5.**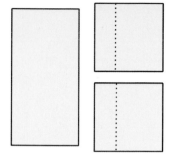

**6.**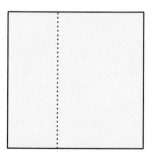

**7.**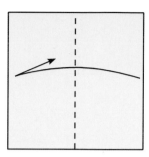

**8.**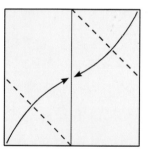

## FOLDING THE MODULES

Begin with a square of one of your chosen colors arranged in the way shown in picture 6.

**6.** The adhesive strip should not be visible.

**7.** Fold in half from right to left, crease firmly, then unfold.

**8.** Fold the top right- and bottom left-hand corners inward using the vertical crease made in step 7 as a guide.

**9.** (*See next page*) Fold the other two corners to the center in a similar way.

**10.** (*See next page*) Unfold all four triangular flaps, but do not open the creases out completely. Look at picture 11.

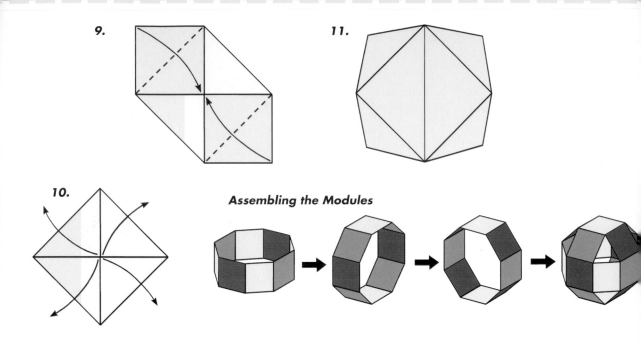

**Assembling the Modules**

**11.** The first module is finished. Make all 18.

### ASSEMBLING THE MODULES

The way to understand how the modules fit together is to look at the underlying structure of the design. This form is made up of 18 square faces and eight triangular ones,

although in this design the triangular faces are missing. It is perhaps easiest to think of it as a combination of three octagonal rings.

**12.** The first two modules go together like this. *Always remember to attach two modules to each other using one completely sticky and one partly sticky flap.*

**13.** Once joined together the flaps always lie on the outside of the assembly.

**14.** This picture shows how the next four modules are added to the assembly. The two modules marked with circles have already been assembled in step 13. Note that all the flaps on all the modules are pointing away from you. Before adding the

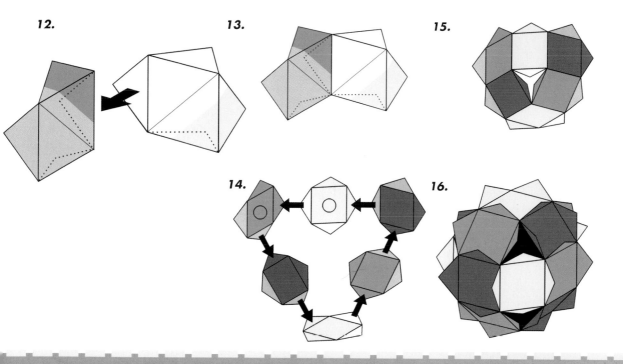

**12.**

**13.**

**14.**

**15.**

**16.**

other modules you should look at picture 15 to see what the result ought to look like. Then look carefully at the way the completely sticky and partly sticky flaps are arranged in relation to each other. In these assembly instructions partly sticky flaps are shaded normally while completely sticky flaps are indicated by lighter shading.

**15.** This is the result. The assembly is concave and all the flaps are arranged on the outside. Continue by adding extra modules in the same way, making sure you keep to the pattern of colors in each of the rings of which the form is made. Again, remember that a completely sticky flap is always stuck to a partly sticky one. If

you follow these instructions the Spiky Ball will form quite automatically as you add the remaining modules.

**16.** When all the modules are in place, work your way around the assembly bringing all the flaps out at the same angle, and making sure the connections between the modules are firm. The Spiky Ball is now complete.

# Flapping Bird

TRADITIONAL DESIGN ADAPTED FOR STICKY NOTES
BY DAVID MITCHELL

Many paperfolders believe that the traditional
Flapping Bird is one of the finest (if not the
finest) origami designs. The design itself,
however, is something of a mystery. While
it is often known as the Japanese Flapping
Bird the design was, until quite recently, little known in Japan. On
the other hand, it is clearly a development of the traditional crane, which is indisputably
Japanese in origin. Wherever it came from, and whenever that was, whoever designed
it has bequeathed the paperfolding community a design to treasure.

The Flapping Bird is folded from a compound square derived from two rectangular
sticky notes. The method by which the compound square is created is given in the
diagrams. The compound square is not of even thickness (some parts are two layers
thick) but you will find that this does not affect the folding procedure. This technique will
also allow you to fold many other origami designs using sticky notes.

**Requirements:** You will need two 3" x 5" (76mm x 127mm) notes. Both notes should
be the same color.

**1.**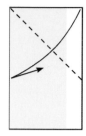

**3.**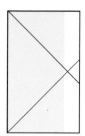

**5.**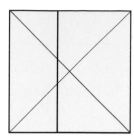

**2.**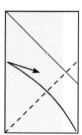

**4.**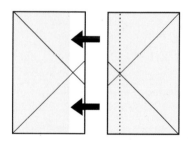

### MAKING THE COMPOUND SQUARE

Begin with a 3" x 5" (76mm x 127mm) note arranged in the way shown in picture 1, so that the adhesive strip is visible.

**1.** Fold the top right-hand corner onto the left-hand edge as shown, crease, then unfold.

**2.** Fold the bottom right-hand corner onto the left-hand edge, crease, then unfold.

**3.** This is the result. Fold both notes to this point then turn one of them over and arrange them in the way shown in picture 4.

**4.** Lay the right-hand note on top of the left-hand note in such a way that both the top and bottom edges, and the diagonal creases, line up. It may take you several attempts to get this right.

**5.** The result should be a perfect compound square. The adhesive strips are both concealed inside the square. Align the square to picture 6.

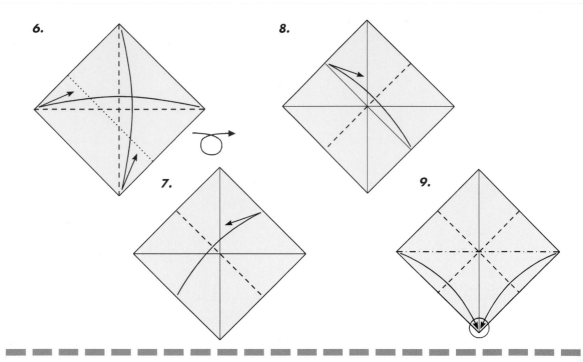

### FOLDING THE FLAPPING BIRD

**6.** Remake the two diagonal creases through all the layers. The line of the join between the two notes is shown here as a dotted line. From here on it will not be shown at all. Turn over sideways.

**7.** Fold in half from edge to edge as shown, crease, then unfold.

**8.** Fold in half from edge to edge in the other direction, crease, then unfold.

**9.** Bring all four corners together (starting with the right and left, and followed by the top) at the point marked with a circle. The square will collapse into the form shown in picture 10.

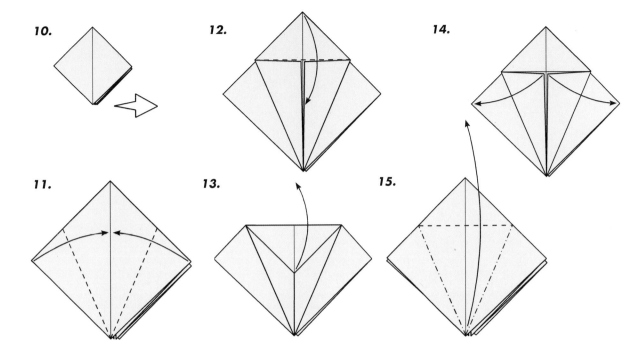

**10.** This is the result. Picture 11 shows this form on a larger scale.

**11.** This form has two layers of flaps on each side. Carefully fold the outside edges of the two front flaps inward to lie along the central crease. Try to make sure that you get sharp points at the bottom.

**12.** Fold the top point downward using the edges of the triangular flaps created in step 11 as a guide. Look at step 13 to see the result. Crease firmly through all the layers.

**13.** Unfold the top point.

**14.** Open out the folds made in step 11.

**15.** Fold the front layer upward using the horizontal crease made in step 12, then flatten the paper using the creases made in step 11 so that the result looks like picture 16. You will not need to make any new creases to do this.

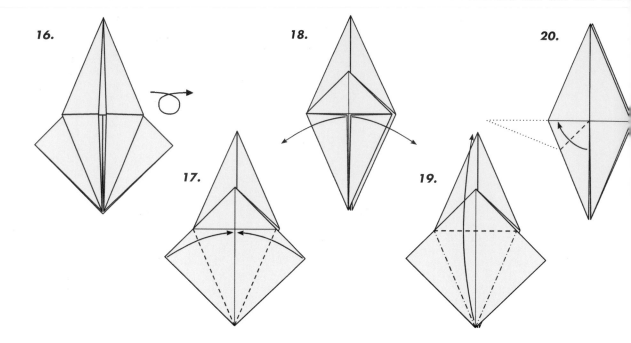

**16.** This is the result. Turn over sideways.

**17.** Fold the outside edges of the two front flaps inward to lie along the central crease. Try to make sure that you get sharp points at the bottom. This is a repeat of step 11.

**18.** Open out the folds made in step 17.

**19.** Fold the front flap upward using the horizontal crease made in step 12, then flatten the paper using the folds made in step 17 so that the result looks like picture 20. You will not need to make any new creases to do this. This is a repeat of step 15.

**20.** There are now two sharply pointed flaps at the bottom. Fold the left-hand flap across to the left, as shown, so that the top of the flap lines up with the horizontal crease made in step 12. The dotted line shows where this flap should end up. Look at picture 21 to see the result.

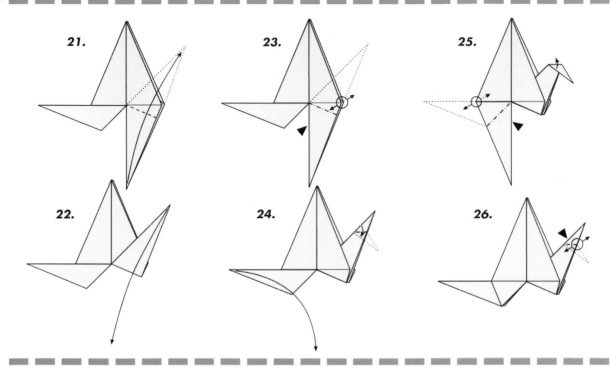

**21.** Fold the right-hand flap upward so that the right-hand edge of the flap is aligned to itself. The dotted line shows where this flap should end up.

**22.** Open out the fold made in step 21.

**23.** Separate the layers at the point identified by a circle and fold the neck up between them using

the creases made in step 21. Note that steps 24 and 25 each contain two separate folding instructions.

**24.** Open out the fold made in step 20 then fold the tip of the right-hand flap downward in the way shown. The dotted line shows where this flap should end up. Look at picture 25 to see the result.

**25.** Separate the layers of the left-hand flap at the point identified by a circle and fold the tail up between them, using the creases made in step 20, then open out the fold made in step 24.

**26.** Separate the layers of the right hand flap at the point identified by a circle and fold the head down between them, using the creases made in step 24.

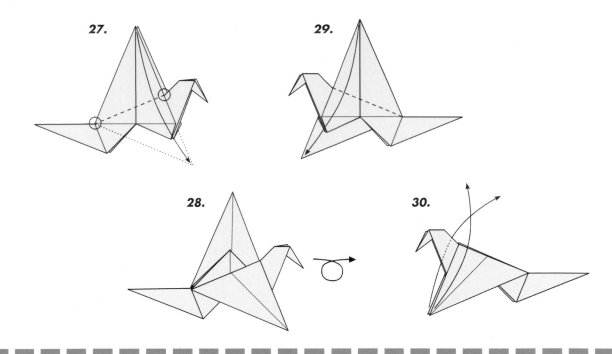

**27.** Fold just the front wing downward as shown. Be careful to make this crease as exactly as possible between the location points identified by circles. The dotted line shows where the wing should end up.

**28.** This is the result. Turn over sideways.

**29.** Repeat step 27 on the other wing. This time you can make the fold accurately by aligning the tip of this wing with the tip of the other.

**30.** Open out the wings to the position shown in picture 31.

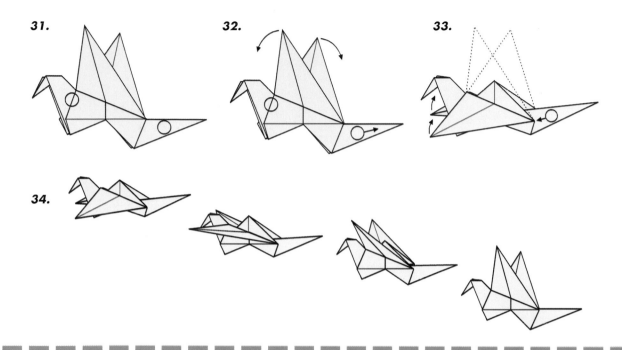

**31.** Take hold of the neck and tail of the bird, between thumb and forefinger of either hand, at the points marked with circles. You should hold the tail with your dominant hand.

**32.** Keep the neck still while pulling gently on the tail. The wings will start to move outward and downward.

**33.** Gently pushing the tail back into position will move the wings upward and inward.

**34.** By alternately pulling and pushing the tail you can make the wings flap repeatedly, as if the bird is in flight.

# Color-Change Collapsible Cube

DESIGNED BY DAVID MITCHELL

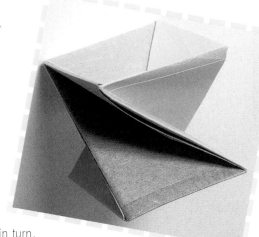

The Color-Change Collapsible Cube is a strangely twisted modular cube that can be flattened and stored in an envelope. With a little practice you will be able to reach into the envelope, and extract the cube in its three dimensional form. A neat trick! Alternatively you can learn to manipulate the cube in the palm of your hand so that, by alternately flattening the cube then opening it out in a new direction, each of the four differently colored modules moves to the front in turn.

Each of the modules is folded from a compound rectangle derived from two square notes attached back to back. The rectangle created from the two squares is known to paperfolders as the Silver Rectangle. It has many intriguing geometrical properties, some of which are utilized in this elegant design. (To make a version of the Cube for left-handers you should follow these instructions in mirror image.)

**Requirements:** You will need eight 3" (76mm) square notes. Ideally you should use two notes of each of four contrasting but complementary colors.

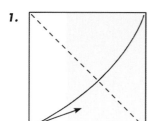

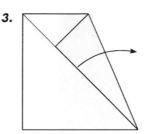

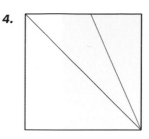

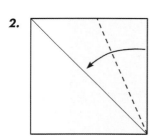

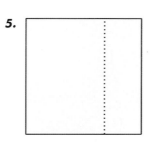

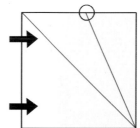

### MAKING A SILVER RECTANGLE

Begin with a 3" (76mm) square note arranged in the way shown in picture 1, so that the adhesive strip is visible.

**1.** Fold in half diagonally, in the way shown, crease firmly, then unfold.

**2.** Fold the right-hand edge inward to lie along the diagonal crease. Try to do this as accurately as possible.

**3.** Open out the fold made in step 2.

**4.** This is the result. You can now attach it to a second square to form a silver rectangle. The second square does not need to be folded at this stage.

**5.** Arrange the two squares like this. The adhesive strip on the left-hand square is not visible but its position is marked by the dotted line. To form the Silver Rectangle lay the left-hand square on top of the right-hand square so that the top and

**6.**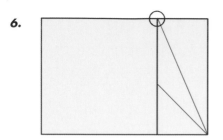

**8.**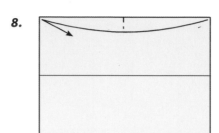

**7.**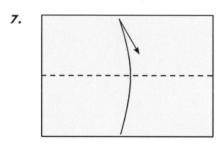

**9.**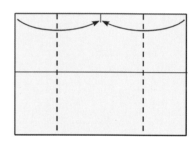

bottom edges line up and the right-hand top corner of the left-hand square is aligned to the point where the crease made in step 2 intersects the top edge of the right-hand square (marked with a circle).

**6.** This is what the Silver Rectangle should look like. Check that the top and bottom edges of the rectangle are straight and that the right-hand edge of the top square is accurately positioned in relation to the crease made in step 2. Adjust if necessary. Note that the adhesive strips of both notes are now concealed inside the rectangle.

Neither the creases made in steps 1 and 2 nor the overlapping edges of the squares will be shown in the pictures from here on.

### FOLDING THE MODULES

**7.** Fold in half from bottom to top, crease, then unfold.

**8.** Make a tiny crease in the center of the top edge by folding one top corner onto the other, then unfold.

**9.** Use the tiny crease made in step 8 as a guide to help you make these two folds.

**10.**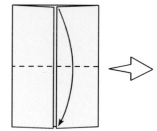

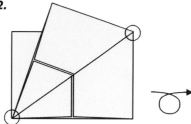 **12.**

**11.**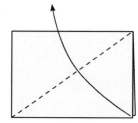

**13.**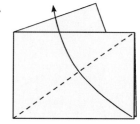

**10.** Fold in half from top to bottom using the crease made in step 7.

**11.** Fold just the front layers in half diagonally, using the bottom left and top right corners to locate the fold. Picture 12 shows what the result should look like.

**12.** Make sure the corners at the end of the crease (marked with circles) are both sharply pointed. Turn over sideways.

**13.** Again, fold just the front layers in half diagonally, using the bottom left and top right corners to locate the fold. Picture 14 shows what the result should look like. This is a repeat of step 11.

**14.**

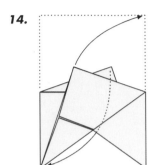

**16.**

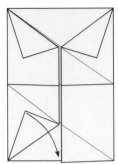

**15.**

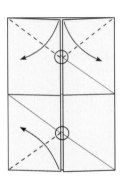

**17.**

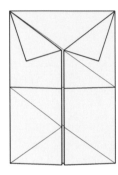

**14.** Open out the creases made in steps 10, 11 and 13.

**15.** Make these three small folds using the outside corners and the intersection of the existing creases with the vertical edges of the paper (marked with circles) as location points.

**16.** Unfold just one of the three folds made in step 15 as shown.

**17.** The module is finished. Make four identical modules using four different colors of notes.

**18.**

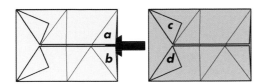

**19.**

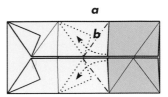

**20.**

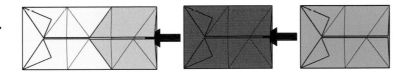

### ASSEMBLING THE COLOR-CHANGE COLLAPSIBLE CUBE

**18.** Align two modules to each other in the way shown here, then insert the left-hand half of one module inside the right-hand half of another. Note the position of flaps **c** and **d** before you slide them inside.

**19.** Fold flaps **a** and **b** inside, beneath flaps **c** and **d** (see picture 18), to lock the modules firmly together. This is difficult, but by no means impossible.

**20.** Repeat steps 18 and 19 as you add the remaining two modules to form a chain.

**21.** (*See next page*) Form the chain into a square section tube by inserting the left-hand module inside the right-hand module. Lock the modules together by repeating step19. This is difficult, but not (absolutely) impossible!

**21.**

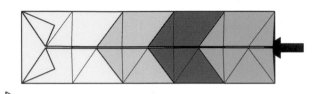

**23.**

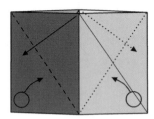

**22.**

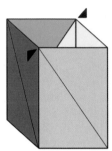

**24.**

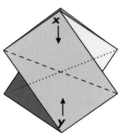

### FORMING THE COLLAPSIBLE CUBE

**22.** This is the result. Squash flat by squeezing two opposite corners together like this.

**23.** Take hold of the two lower corners of the flattened tube with your right and left hands at the points marked with circles. Gently rotate your hands toward each other in the direction of the arrows so that the model collapses into the form shown in picture 24.

**24.** Separate the front and back layers at the top and bottom. Hold the model between your thumb and index finger at points **x** and **y**. Gently squeeze the points toward each other.

**25.** The cube is formed. You can collapse it by reversing step 24 in either direction (front to back or left to right) and store it in an envelope. With a little practice you will be able to reach into the envelope and extract the cube in its three dimensional form. You can also learn to manipulate the cube as a color changer, as shown in pictures 26 through 28.

**25.**

**27.**

**26.**

**28.**

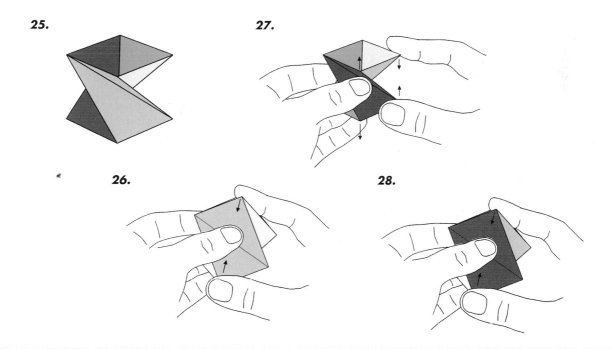

### THE COLOR CHANGER

**26.** To work the color changer, flatten the cube and hold it loosely in your left hand. With your right thumb and index finger separate the front and back layers at both the top and the bottom of the model. Squeeze the points toward

each other to form the cube. Relax the grip of your left hand as you do this and allow the model to rotate to the right.

**27.** Now use your left thumb to flatten the cube so that the second colored face replaces the first at the front of the model.

**28.** If you are careful not to flatten the model completely you will find it easy to transfer your right thumb and index finger to the new top and bottom corners and to repeat steps 18 and 19 to bring the third colored face into view. You will soon find it easy to rotate all four colored faces in this way.

# Acknowledgments

My grateful thanks are due to my friends Jenny and Martyn for lending me their home to work and relax in, Sue and Tung Ken for ideas and inspiration, Frances, Chris and Adam for access to their broadband connection and Annie for showing me how you learn to walk.

## *GOING FURTHER WITH ORIGAMI*

Information about many other interesting aspects of origami can be found at the author's website: www.origamiheaven.com

There are dedicated origami clubs in many countries, which arrange meetings and publish magazines and collections of new designs. The two main English speaking clubs are the British Origami Society and Origami USA, both of which are non-profit organizations run by volunteers. Both clubs have a worldwide membership base.

Origami USA can be contacted through www.origami-usa.org
The British Origami Society can be contacted through www.britishorigami.org.uk